the che diaries

The true story of personal transformation, healing and love from out of this world!

by: AVE GUEVARA

Cover Photos by Waking Crow Studios
Cover Design by Robbi Spencer, SE Studios

Library of Congress Cataloging-in-Publication Data is available from the Library of Congress.

Catalogue Data Pending.

Published 2014 Sacred Grove Publishing
13344 Grass Valley Avenue, Suite G
Grass Valley, California 95945

SACRED GROVE
PUBLISHING

The Che Diaries – Second Edition
ISBN #: 978-1502337764
Printed in the United States of America

THIS BOOK IS DEDICATED TO

THE "FORCE OF SOURCE" ~ THE CREATOR

AND TO ALL PEOPLE WHO'S INTENTION IS TO AWAKEN

TO THEIR PURPOSE AND CREATIVE POWER WITHIN

* * *

"An invisible thread connects those who are destined to meet, regardless of time, place and circumstance. The thread may stretch or tangle. But it will never break."

-Ancient Chinese Proverb

THE CHE DIARIES

INTRODUCTION

At the moment my eyes first met the old black and white image of Che Guevara in Argentina, the dormant fires of a destiny between us ignited full flame. That first glance awakened **us** and he charged into my soul with the fierceness of a chariot in battle. He *commanded my attention,* changing the course of my life in an instant. This life course expanded every aspect of my life, awakening me to my empowerment as a healer and my previously misunderstood gift as a multi-dimensionally empathic sensitive.

Recognizing 'the presence' *after* the trip, in my home, intensified his energy. The times we co-habitated in my body *together,* lasted only moments but will linger always. A door opened wider than I thought possible expanding my mind, pushing me beyond all limits in my conscious and subconscious mind. At random times our union would transport me into a state of ecstasy beyond literal description.

Nothing looks the same. I crossed through the doorway into a different room, never to return to my original frame of thinking. This unexpected companion wreaked havoc in my life initially, but the purpose of our union eventually revealed itself beyond question.

Expansion and being awakened to one's true purpose can at first wreak havoc with what we've already had set in motion if we are not living in harmony with what our true purpose is.

So strong came the direction to publish these notes and messages received from the non-physical dimension, I **COULDN'T** ignore it.

"Are you kidding??? Take my private notes from this mind blowing experience and put it out to the world??? No way!!"

Since being a tiny child yet unable to speak, I clearly remember the awareness of a specific 'mission' linked to this new life. Communications from 'the other side' have always guided me with a strong sense of purpose. It was something I always just *knew*. In digesting the environment with my new sensory receptors at that young age, I remember thinking communication here was rather archaic.

PREFACE

My arrival in Buenos Aires coincided with the 39th anniversary of the execution of Che Guevara. At this time, I was unaware of both this anniversary and the revolutionary's infamous existence.

Historically, I've consciously experienced two visits with beings from non-physical. Both times I had close relationships with children whose mother had died when they were young. When the deceased mother 'asked' if she could hug her child *through* my arms just to *feel* them, this seemed a natural request. These visits validated the reality of the spirit not dying just because the body expires, and feeling her presence *in with mine* felt like a holy experience, not weird or scary. There are beings living among us whose life force vibrates at a frequency rendering them invisible to mortal eyes. But they *can* be felt and they convey messages we can 'receive' and understand. It's not like hearing voices in your head that control you, possess you and make you do weird stuff.

I didn't pursue a career offering this service, nor did I tell anyone *or* contemplate it as some phenomenon. I just allowed the brief visits and wrote about them in my journal. In my first experience with the mother of four children and three grandchildren, she shifted from a sense of transmitting gratitude to me for allowing her presence within me to becoming rather pushy about her visits. As soon as it became uncomfortable, I said, "ENOUGH!" and her visits ceased.

I have learned that the existence of this aspect of creation is not contingent upon a human belief system. It simply IS. Some people are just more sensitive, some minds more open. Belief systems have a way of closing people's minds to the fullness of Creation when it involves something out of the perception of ordinary. I learned too, that people like to judge others as 'crazy' when their experiences suggest there's more to life than their belief systems allow, keeping them locked in their tiny little comfort zones.

Always one to think *outside the box* found me the recipient of some very uncomfortable, judgmental situations. Now, *I LIVE* outside the box, and I feel right at home.

A gift for all who read this book:

You, the reader will be blessed as the words on these pages are infused with the intent for your spiritual expansion and well-being.

Ave infuses her art, music & literary works with a high vibrational essence. Hence, you receive the gift of being uplifted and expanded as you are exposed to her creative arts.

⋆ THE JOURNEY BEGINS ⋆

PRELUDE TO MEETING CHE:
OPENING & EMPTYING OF MIND

I arrived in this country at death's door. In a state so weakened from throwing my guts up throughout the flights, I was barely able to walk off the plane. Arriving in the long line to enter Argentina, I was crumbled on the floor using my suitcase to prop me up, crawling slowly as the line inched forward. I could not stand up. Did I come here to die?

7 Octubre

This death-like illness was my body's reaction to the extreme stress of having discovered en route my former partner was legally pulling the rug out from under me. I was heading to a needed vacation to clear my mind from the painful dissolution of that union, and focus on what my new life was going to be. I sensed a strong shift was to occur, but didn't remotely fathom what was before me. If the end result from the time I spend in this country has any relation to the condition in which I arrived, then I could be in for one helluva transformation. Time to jump in. We shall see.

8 Octubre

"I am HERE!! In the city of Buenos Aires!"

Arriving in Argentina is like stepping into *another world,* another *ME*! My inner adventurer has been retrieved and awakened! My 'core' erupts to life like a volcano.

I AM FALLING IN LOVE WITH ME!!!!

This love affair starts *today*! I am meeting this new improved being right here in *Argentina,* and bringing ME home to MYSELF.

"Holy smokes, I'm in a different HEMISPHERE!!! This is a first.

Immersed within a different culture and language beneath a different night sky, my sense of wonder becomes wide open and I am saturated with the beautiful feeling of *absolute freedom.*

9 Octubre

For one who rarely cries, I've had bouts of this emotional cleansing since being here, as has my traveling friend. We came here together as compadres on vacation; to reinvent *ourselves* and discover the new direction life holds for us, as we are each at personal crossroads. We assist each other with our introspections and resurrections, sharing long talks and spilling our guts. Tears cleanse our souls then we launch into bursts of laughter. So far, this vacation does not fit the definition of one, but seems like a workshop of self-discovery in an exotic location.

I *will* undergo a major transformation in this country and *will* not return to life as it *was.* The youthful spirit of rebelliousness beckons, accompanied by that strong sense of purpose.

As she knows me to be forever restless, my mother wishes after this trip, I would return to my cabin in the woods finding contentment with a 'normal' job. I sat with this request and wish I could live with that simplistic wish, but it would *kill* me. Surviving mediocrity is not an option. I've always had a strong sense of purpose behind this life and restlessness was a constant companion, as I had not yet uncovered this true purpose. I sense I am onto it now however, like a hound on the scent! It feels so close I can *smell* it! **My quest *will* be revealed here in *this* country!**

I don't even relate to my *name* anymore, don't 'feel' like the person who left California. My return home will encompass changes so profound I sense my name will *change*. A rebirth is imminent. My personal revolution has begun... I feel as if I'm resonating at a different frequency!

When framing my environment through the lens of my camera, I lose myself (whoever *that* is!) into the act of *seeing*. It's a beautiful escape from the mind. To *be* and not *think* is liberating.

15 Octubre

Just returned from a solo adventure to the Recoleta. Today felt like a *real vacation*. I touched ancient coffins through their broken glass enclosures, and pet feral cats that reside in great numbers at the famed cemetery.

A solo expedition in this country with my camera is the ultimate fun. Nightfall finds me entering the Lady of Pilar church for the local's mass. The children's choir sang harmonies with classical guitars, moving me into the realm of angels. I sat up front allowing the transport of my soul to hover outside myself.

17 Octubre

To Le Catedral (The Cathedral). One of my passions is immersing myself within historic structures and cemeteries. Be they ancient ruins or majestic cathedrals, capturing photographic images and feeling the vibration of occupants long gone is compelling. I was primed with a sense of awe and wonder, setting me up for what was to follow...

There were many altars to the Virgin and Christ. My friend and I found ourselves within the innermost sanctum of this enormous architectural wonder. It was a small altar hidden behind the main one, which was of a height and expanse that seemed to touch heaven itself! This space issued forth profound holiness, and countless prayers resonated through me. Not being religious did not deter us from meditating at the feet of the crucified Christ where we lost our sense of self. Ours was the 'religious experience' one reads of *others* having. When mi compadre and I looked at each other after an unknown lapse of time, tears were streaming from our blank staring eyes; we both were deeply entranced.

Silently, we made our way to the noisy streets in this altered state, catching a cab to our apartment. The evening passed in a state of emptiness I found comforting. Schubert's hymn, 'Ave Maria' played in my head for hours after this rendezvous with Spirit. Inside and out, the dramatic melody resonated within the total emptiness of my being.

18 Octubre
4:30 AM

Humbled to lying in the darkness releasing emotion for so long, I find myself to be a hollow frame from the explosion of life I once thought myself to be. Bursting with optimism to give my gifts to the world inspiring those of lesser hope, it is I who's dreams lay in the recesses of what might have been and seems to be no more. It is I, with no dreams left as I remain in the state of complete emptiness.

There is no doubt yesterday's experience en Le Catedral has emptied my mind and heart to receive something more profound than fulfillment of human yearnings. The scent strengthens as I sense I am on to *something.*

22 Octubre
Sunday Morning

Adventurer's ecstasy was mine in the back seat of Ricardo's taxi yesterday as he sang along to his radio blasting Italian opera. Happily, he whizzed us through heavy traffic as if it were a dance. As joyful the effect the weaving cab had upon *me,* it sickened my trusty companion. Redirecting my bliss into broken Spanish I explained her condition to our 'chauffeur'. Ricardo veered immediately from the intended route speeding off where only he seemed to know. With a flash of taxi savvy on safety, my gut told me this guy could be trusted, as we had previously engaged in fun conversation and his friendliness was genuine.

We arrived at his cousin's auto garage in a dilapidated old neighborhood. Ricardo fetched water and tended to my friend with the concerned attention of a hovering parent anxious for their child's recovery while speaking rapid Spanish to his cousin.

Ricardo told his cousin of my wish to learn tango. Gustavo, a tall, elegant gentleman, just happened to be a tango instructor when not selling used cars. Immediately he played some tango music, took me in his arms and showed me the steps. The scene was straight out of a movie; nestled in Gustavo's crushing embrace, I followed his smooth moves gliding across the cement floor of his immaculate garage amidst a sea of old vehicles. This hospitable gentleman offered me free lessons and assistance in my purchase of tango shoes. We made a date to meet where locals purchase their tango gear and Ricardo would drive. "You cannot dance without proper shoes!" he insisted emphatically in melodious Spanish. *This* is Argentina!

⋆ PIGEONS, TANGO & CHE ⋆

23 Octubre

With separate notes and many photos, I am chronicling the life of a pigeon family roosting on the ledge across from our apartment. Each morning I creep to the window unnoticed by the feathered family, snapping many pictures and writing my observations. The chicks begin flying exercises under parental supervision. I'm inspired while spying this scene to transform their life into a children's book. *Nobody ever sees a baby pigeon!* I watch them every morning, growing from tiny yellow chicks to miniature pigeons, running back and forth on the ledge preparing for flight.

It feels refreshing to have creative inspiration awakened and give me direction to write and illustrate a book from this study I've undertaken.

My first tango lesson with Gustavo went well. Initially, it felt like my feet were two left fins on the back of a fish out of water. With Gustavo's encouragement and velvety patience, I became comfortable with the steps and felt the flow of this passionate dance. In Argentina tango is not just a dance, but a religion.

My friend and I went to La Boca, birthplace of tango. We walked around the street fair and enjoyed a great lunch seated at a table in the middle of a cobblestone street.

La Boca's buildings once brilliantly painted, were peeled and fading. The streets were closed to traffic, accommodating the crowds. The rest of the neighborhood was closed to tourists and none were allowed to walk outside the designated area. Learning this to be a dangerous barrio added mystique to a place already filled with intrigue.

I stared beyond the blockades into the forbidden neighborhood longing to walk those streets and merge with the locals. I felt myself as belonging *there* and not among the tourists.

Vendors lined the streets selling miniature tango shoes and anything tango one could imagine. *The sacred dance was a commercial industry!* Enamored with the endless sea of unique artifacts, I was momentarily disgusted at my gringo status seduced by this commercialism. The atmosphere was happy and light evaporating this sentiment somewhat. The parade of street musicians filled the air with lively sounds of Latino music. Behind the lens of my camera, I was again overflowing with the effervescent wonder of a child. My body tingled with the sparkle of life and I blended into the scene. I was comfortable with the sense of being between worlds, belonging nowhere and being nobody.
With my camera, I feel more like an artist than a tourist.

His picture in a distant store window drew me over to it with an immediate sense of urgency. I had no idea who he was as I stood frozen and overcome with a sense of recognition on a level that was unfathomable. I stared with a sense of abandon that jolted me far outside myself. The noise of the surrounding crowds pushing all around me evaporated, my sense of self dissolved. I had never experienced anything like this.

So, was the first moment my eyes met with Ernesto Che Guevara.

The image held me riveted where I stood. *Who was this guy?* Eventually my trusty companion pulled me into the store, but not out of my transcendent state. Once inside, still transfixed and unable to ignore the strength of a connection that had overtaken me, I gazed upon an assortment of black and white photo cards of this same man.

It was not unlike meeting a stranger who upon that meeting, feel like you've *always* known. This meeting, however, had the added intensity that grabbed and twisted me inside and out. These were *just photographs*, and their effect upon me was too intense to be ignored. I was moved to purchase several cards and restrained myself from purchasing *all* of them. I could not break away from the stand displaying these pictures—remaining adhered to the spot. I was compelled to linger and bask in the warmth of this connection that had me entranced, removing me entirely from present reality.

Eventually leaving, I walked partially in the current world, and mostly in some other world.

I couldn't shake the feeling that was awakened in me and felt coerced to take out the postcards I'd purchased gazing at him. I was mesmerized. With each glance, part of me transported elsewhere while walking among the crowds in La Boca. I was amused listening to my friend saying I was possessed. Both her joking and her presence were blurred in some distance far from wherever I was. I indeed felt *something* was taking place other than a possession or obsession over a face on some old pictures that were no doubt touched up.

I met Che Guevara in La Boca, birthplace of tango, surrounded by the spirit of the historic dance and its subsequent commercialization.

24 Octubre
4:30 A.M.

<u>DREAM</u>: Engaged in the fervor of a most captivating tango connection, I was enslaved by the passion behind the strength of the embrace and the penetration of the gaze of my partner's eyes into mine. Our bodies were fluid and moved as one. The color, the emotion between us, and the feeling from that dream stays brighter in wakefulness than the sun's reflection dancing on water. My partner was the man on the images who only yesterday, connected with me on the streets of La Boca, Señor Guevara.

27 Octubre

"Glory comes through struggle"—Che
   Then I must be pretty glorious, with all my struggling years as a single mom.

My 'partner in crime' presented me with information on Guevara obtained at the "locutorio"- a room on the corner of every city block with phones and computer booths for public use. She also brought information on Iguazu Falls, one of the world's wonders we intend to explore.

"I have a sense that the days as I knew them are ending, and that something new is waiting beyond the burnt edges of the pages of my life."

This excerpt is from the novel, "Loving Che", by Ana Menendez, and the quote rings true to my soul and logical mind the *instant* my eyes take it in.

I enjoyed a solo adventure to the bookstore previously discovered on one of our many walks around the city. My intent was to linger there a long time, as to be in the company of books is one of my favorite activities, and like tango does not interest my friend. I found this book in a remote pile beneath a ladder and purchased the novel in full judgment of the book by its cover. A lovely design with a photograph of my new 'heart-throb' (as we have laughingly started to call him), *and* it was in *English. No muchos libros en Ingles.*

I learned that Señor Guevara was as much an icon during his era as the beloved Princess Diana was in her time, but for different reasons of course. They had followings of those that adored and those that were threatened by them, and were controversial figures possessing film star looks. Knowing anything about each of these individuals beyond this is obtained only through the propaganda machine called the media.

He was the epitome of a hero, and this status is all the information available. I am compelled to learn more about him upon my return to the states. After several days, the intensity of the tango dream still accompanies me. My friend pokes fun at my being obsessed with him, and I laugh along with her, knowing it's not obsession. We joke that my new boyfriend is a 'dead revolutionary'.

The connection I feel with the spirit of this person goes deeper than the image of him, and I find it strange and disconcerting, as behind the joking it feels like there's actually *something to this.* I've never been a groupie for rock stars, athletes, celebrities, *or* revolutionaries.

This is different.

☆ DREAMS, DEATH & TANGO ☆

29 Octubre

<u>DREAM</u>: Details are unclear and fade with trying to recall them. But the feeling of being absolutely madly in love, and it being returned to me with the same intensity was crystal clear, and that part has stayed with me. The ecstasy of feeling this love and sharing it with one who loved me equally was the core of the dream. I did not want to wake from this. His face was crystal clear. It was the face of Señor Guevara.

True my thoughts no doubt brought this dream on, I contest not the possibility and probability of this. Point is, the dream occurred and added to the sense of something awakening, as had my initial glimpses of his photographs and the tango dream. Maybe our dream state is what's real, and when we awaken to consciousness we are actually in the illusory dream state. We only *identify* with what *seems* like 'real life'. How would we know it to be different?

What is actually the truth is irrelevant, and my mind is open to all possibilities. Being mindful of not reading too much into either these dreams or this bizarre occurrence over his photos, I avoid belief systems that impose limitations, and will put him out of my mind.

Last night held the excitement of pounding rain and thunderstorms. Blinding flashes of light followed by deafening thunder vibrated the windows. *I LOVED it!* Still sleepy, I stirred awake entertaining the acquisition of a puppy after this vacation. I need a pleasant distraction from solo living and this constant work on my*self.* Life on the spiritual path can be unnerving, tiresome and terrifying. This is the flip side of what also bestows bliss and clarity, even if that bliss only lasts moments few and far between. An occasional distraction from all of this is quite possibly the best medicine I could hope for. Puppies are synonymous with distraction.

I find myself actually feeling lifted from the fear of meeting someone and falling in love. Maybe I really *do* want romantic love and *marry again*! My cynicism on romance and marriage may be lightening up as my heart heals from past wounds. These thoughts surprise me but my heart feels somehow lighter. The storm may have affected me more than just taking delight in its intensity.

I get a feeling I just *might* meet the love of my life, my soul partner, right *here* in South America! I always sensed the partner I was born to be with wasn't even *on* this planet after so much heartbreaker love in my own country. *Maybe I was just on the wrong continent.*

31 Octubre
6:30 A.M.

The dream has accompanied me vividly even after two days pass; a fierce love awakened, deep and strong, with an aliveness of spirit that has captured my full attention. There have now been two emotionally charged dreams that feel more potent than illusionary lingerings. The significance of dreams being debatable, it's the *intensity* and *feeling* of these dreams that hold the significance. Perhaps it's just my own fantasies lived out while I safely sleep, nothing more. We shall see.

It could be a past life memory surfacing if we indeed lived before, who knows - anything is possible. In my current life, his life as Che is insignificant. I realize he was an icon, but it is not his icon status that comes to mind when I feel this connection. It is an awakening with the spirit, not the man. There seems to be more to this and it's worthy of at least maintaining an open mind.

It's rather an intrigue than a passing crush on a photo of unattainable love. I choose to be only a witness to its effect on me and not give it too much thought.

2 Noviembre
Maybe life is just a series of adjustments to cycles and phases then *PUFF*, the cycle gives way to something distant from the human scope of understanding or imagination. Do we ever *not* wonder anymore? Does wonder create a longing to *know?* Can I not just *BE*, without this *longing?* Does longing dam up the flow of happiness? Is longing a tool that serves to awaken me to my purpose? What is happiness but contentment with what *IS?* Am I discontent because I fear it would remove my drive in the accomplishment of the purpose? Is a sense of purpose the ultimate coyote? Where is the handbook to guide me in the use of my restlessness properly for the highest good? Do I fear being an unfulfilled homeless old beggar, dying a painful death utterly alone? Is the drive to accomplish something merely an ingrained societal belief system?

Do I fear most of all not fulfilling the mission I was born to accomplish due to ongoing human distractions? I feel a nudge from something that is *way* bigger than me, my life, or what I think my dreams are. Time to explore what's behind this nudge. Training wheels are off and I'm riding the motorbike of life! The wind is blasting my face and with no fear of falling, **I'm simply *riding!!*** Life may be a bike, or a surfboard... one never knows when one will *catch that wave*, but when you do, you stand up and **ride with all you've got.** Ride to the end, applying skill and grace that comes with experience to not wipe out before the ride is over. I regard my life as that wave; my grace and balance are developing enough to stand up and ride with complete joy and exhilaration. Occasional wipeouts are expected on this path with face plants in the sand and gulping for air beneath the surf, fumbling and tumbling. Then I come to understand, **the ride goes on forever!**

Later that Same Day...

"Bird Down"

One of the pigeon chicks died in the nest and the sibling will not leave its side. Flying lessons have ceased; the parent birds patiently sit on the opposite side of the ledge looking at the nest, as the defensive little chick will not let them near. When a parent approaches, the chick flaps its wings in frenzy, leaning forward to be threatening. Chirping as quickly and loudly as it can, it's *definitely* upset. This has gone on for a few days. It saddens me a bit seeing this baby bird in such grief, yet I'm assuming the position as observer of what happens in the natural world humans don't get to see every day. This opportunity is a gift of sorts, despite the discomfort I feel from my observations.

This will make *some* story for *kids!* Why can't the birds just live happily ever after? Why can't the two chicks learn to fly, get on with their lives, and live a story I can write that goes something like the perfect fairy tale life doesn't seem to be?

5 Noviembre
1:00 A.M.

Just returned home from a solo trip to the 'tango cauldron'. I call it such because it was like being *in* one; a crowded combination of human ingredients all mixed together forming a steaming dish with strong Latin American flavor in a well seasoned old pot (the basement dance hall).These were lessons for locals, not a tourist tango extravaganza—the teacher barks out directions in rapid Spanish and I understood nothing, nada. Only one person spoke a tidbit of Ingles. Panic hit several times and I felt like bolting out of the place. I was pleased with hanging in there, slaying the fear dragons. Victorious and on my own, I was able to check my jacket, purchase chewing gum and get around the dance floor with an assortment of characters. The crowd began to thicken after the lesson ended, people gathering to drink and dance. When the small Peruvian man who was my last partner wanted to buy me beer but went out for a smoke first, I quickly changed from tango shoes and bolted.

The freshness and freedom of the outside, escaping from what became a very crowded dance hall, enlivened and recharged me as I drank in the crisp night air beneath the street lamps. I began a fast pace through the cobblestone streets passing sidewalk cafes with a smorgasbord of different characters. They leisured at tables drinking wine and coffee, engaged in their conversations and merriment, the sound being a mixture of different languages. Moving through all this joyful activity was contagious; feeling free and on my own, I was in high spirits with zest in my veins and bounce in my step.

I turned down a street toward the neighborhood that was familiar from the many long walks my friend and I have taken since being here. The street people were everywhere, meticulously going through all the curbside garbage. Some were families with small children and babies, and many were solo men, bedraggled, dirty and working hard at collecting bits and pieces of everything imaginable they could find some use for or to eat. They had soulful brown eyes and pulled their huge homemade carts; some piled as high as eight or ten feet, their burden covered with ratty old tarps. There seemed to be an air of routine to this sub-culture of people that are rarely seen during the day.

At night, the neighborhoods took on a different life. I never felt threatened as I walked the streets with a brisk sense of purpose, my tango shoes in their bag slung over my shoulder, my senses fully alert. The apartment lobbies all lit up reminded me of a series of different paintings with their individual expressions of texture, angles, color and carefully placed plants. Each apartment and storefront had its own style of sidewalks as well, a different stone, or textured concrete. Some glistened beneath the street lamps having been freshly washed off, some were lifted and cracked from the knarly roots of old trees pushing up from beneath. It was like walking through a 3-D art gallery of life. One always has to be conscious of the numerous piles left by dogs at any time day or night.

Approaching my apartment I saw a young street mother with two young sons and a tiny girl. She rummaged through the trash, her children well behaved and patient with the ritual. My heart broke when my gaze met with the big brown eyes of the little girl peering up at me. Unsure if I would offend the pride of this young woman, I handed her a fistful of pesos while whispering humble blessings. In her native tongue, she blessed me with gratitude, tears welling up in her eyes. I wanted to hug her, invite her into my home and feed the children a bowl of cereal. I arrived to my room tired yet exhilarated with a warm feeling of 'mission accomplished brave warrior'. I'm off to sleep with a smile on my face and a crack in my heart for that beautiful young mother, her children, and all those families digging through trash out on the streets.

Later that day . . .

Traffic sounds seem 'easier' on Sunday mornings, my watch ticking loudly beside my bed and the birds vague in their song. Buses GRIND with a grating noise and loud engines overrule interspersed with squeaky brakes, jolting me out of my early morning peace. My companion remains blissfully asleep in the next room.

It will be fun to re-read these pages someday. Pero cuando?

I love speaking Spanish, and am delighted by sidewalk life and the dog walkers. Greyhounds always lead the pack, pit bulls always muzzled, the little yipper dogs run along to keep up. These packs of dogs are as part of the landscape as the cafes.

Flower sellers on the corners emanate charm and color. Fresh baked bread piled high in huge baskets perfectly balanced atop the person's head riding their bicycle to the local vendor amazes me. Leaving a trail of the bread's fresh, warm scent piques my senses as I breathe it in. The meat vendor is a lovely man whom I've come to know after photographing him standing proudly beside his butchered cow. He waves to me and yells, "!Hola, que tal?" every time I pass. "Bien, gracias, y vos?" is my reply, the standard greeting between familiars. **I feel like a local.**

We will be catching a cab today to San Antonio de Areca. Adventure time...Yip e e e e e!

Che postcards, Che calendar—*what was I thinking?* Good looking probably, dead- - *absolutely.*
He simply does not stay out of my mind and will pop in on me at random moments.

A bit later that same day . . .

The parent birds turned the dead chick into a featherbed by covering it with twig grass and stomping it down into the nest - not a good visual for a children's book. Then they sat upon the new 'featherbed' and laid an egg. The surviving chick seems content with this situation and they seem to be getting on with their pigeon lives. Turning this scene into the happy ending that has transpired so far will take some work to make it palatable for children while maintaining the integrity of the event.

Freshly caffeinated from our morning jo' and energized from fresh squeezed orange juice, we await a cab coming to take us on a field trip. San Antonio de Areca calls to me. Heavy, low, gray clouds promise a rainy adventure. My trusty companion indulges me this trip, she isn't thrilled about it and thinks me loco for being 'drawn' to this remote place. The buzzer sounds, signaling the cabs arrival---here we go!!!

★ ADVENTURES WITHIN & OUT ★

6 Noviembre

We drove what seemed *forever* to that tiny town of no tourists! This was the local's biggest day staging their annual parade. With camera in face, there was a break in the rains as I photographed costumed people of all ages riding beautifully groomed horses through the neighborhood streets.

The rain poured as we drove around, and the cabbie became our 'good friend' assuming the role of personal tour guide. He had never been out this far from the city throughout his taxi career, and he was jovial and fun loving the entire time. He had such good spirits that he turned off the meter as we drove the narrow streets.

Our lunch experience was the kind of blast one has outside of anything familiar. I imbibed my first glass of local wine, best I've *ever tasted*. We shared much laughter and stories and with no other patrons, were given personal attention like old friends. Such is the warmth of Argentina! We returned home tired from the long ride, but again, I was exhilarated as always after any adventure.

7 Noviembre
before sunrise

Sparkling in remote grooves of my mind, hints the thought that I am outgrowing my name and will be stepping into another. After the experience in Le Catedral, the resonant sound (aka: name) that feels harmonious to my spirit is Ave (pro: Ah'vay). I walked out from the rapture not *feeling* like Kari anymore, my essential frequency shifted.

Keeping my surname, de Velasco, is set in stone (if anything on earth has that certain a fate), but there is another name lurking in the depths of my mind. I will let this simmer in my subconscious allowing the right name to surface at the right time. Assuming a new name is a shift that requires stillness, clarity and time to simmer.

Later that same day . . .

I am tired and empty of words.
* * *

Ariel and Carlos. The kiss 'attack' on the corner from the latter who didn't even ask my name, and the affectionate attentions from the former who is very kind but whiney, unattractive and has never seen a toothbrush. **Why have these two characters been attracted to me??**

Ariel manages one of the nicer uptown locutorios, gives me free internet time, little candies and sweet glances betraying his attraction. Carlos works in the café near our apartment, we're always passing the place and stopping in for coffee and fresh juice. Time for a different café!

After accepting Ariel's invitation for coffee and conversation, I see clearly the judgments I've held of this kind person with entirely different reference points due to cultural differences. His young life does not contain support for big ambitions.

My kindness is actually the highlight in his daily mundane duties of living with his mother and younger siblings, holding employment that is nothing more than a way to pay the household bills. His job helps support them, and although he dreams of becoming a doctor, there is little hope he will ever be able to leave that job to attend medical school long enough to earn his degree, as his father left the family to fend for themselves. They depend on Ariel's income and leaving them for any reason is not an option.

My North American attitude expanded to embrace more compassion after experiencing shame from my prejudgments. His life leaves no time to think of things like the importance of proper brushing or dental floss. I am careful not to behave in any manner leading him to believe my friendliness contains any personal attraction.

Without a doubt, it's time to escape the city and get to the Iguazu wilderness. An extended stay in the jungle is the elixir my soul needs immediately! The big city has been stimulating, fascinating and different, but it's time to be surrounded by the force and power of Mother Nature. When I return home, things will be different for this new person I feel awakening within. I possess a sense of excitement about what is on the other side of this journey. I am growing into my expansion. Arriving home to my sanctuary in the *jungles* of California, I will learn how to *enjoy* doing what it takes to take *good* care of myself. Caring always first for others, be they the children or the partner, I have neglected the aspect of genuine self-care. God *is* this body/mind system that I inhabit, and by loving and nurturing *me*, I do so for that which created me. I will rid from my life those whose involvement with me is destructive. I will focus my intent on self-empowerment and relieve myself from the stresses I have courted so long, shaking them off like the bad habits that they are and have been. As fears arise to disturb my peace, I will release them and surround myself only with true friends. Learning to see the positive and good in everyone is to free myself from negativity in the form of perceptions, opinions or judgments. Ah, time for breakfast!

8 Noviembre

What's with these thoughts popping up about being the baby of well-known, wealthy parents? They have no basis from anything I've read, heard or dreamed about, and at random times come to me like a déjà vu. I'll just let the thought flow arise and float by, observe it without contemplation.

Singer, songwriter, artist, musician, photographer, illustrator, garden designer, writer...why am I ALL these things and not just one or two? It is IMPOSSIBLE to focus on just one of those arts and do IT only. It's like having more than one child and being expected to love and nurture only one of them. I cannot fathom this. Writing and illustrating the Pigeon Chronicles will be a primary focus, and to get the book FINISHED. Give the other facets of myself up entirely in order to accomplish this? I can't see myself doing that! I can't NOT play my violin or guitar, and I can't NOT put my hands in the dirt. And I certainly can't work on just one painting at a time and ignore my love of photography. If only I didn't need to sleep! My challenge is to COMPLETE a project, as my interests are so vast! I only wish the next lifetime could pick up where this one leaves off and I get to continue all my studies, delving deeper and perfecting what I've spent this present life learning.

The zest of anticipating a new day seems to have morphed into detached observations. Although I perceive myself as lacking enthusiasm, others perceive me as having plenty, am I still being really hard on myself and cutting me no slack? Ah, the eternal PROCESS.

Perhaps what I perceive as zestlessness is an actual achievement to the status of detached observer, having believed enthusiasm is followed by disappointment. Fewer ups and downs seem a more productive existence as we humans get addicted to the ups, and medicate to get through the downs. Or this could be just one of those old belief systems that no longer serve my highest good! So it seems.

Growing pains become adolescent emotional upheavals-becomes heartbreak of unrequited crushes-becomes cramps and confusion of the childbearing cycle beginning-becomes PMS- becomes fear of loss-becomes survival-becomes heartbreak when my little girl cries for a father wondering why he doesn't want to know her- becomes perimenopause and all the symptoms of reproductive system upheaval-becomes heartache from unrequited love relationships throughout adulthood-becomes menopause and the personal journey into uncontrollable hot flash, mood-swing hell-becomes empty nest-becomes grief from tragic death within the family of a pregnant young woman in her prime-becomes depression- becomes totally broken down-becomes seeker of recovery. Becomes authentic. My authenticity allows appreciation of having lived through, expanded and become empowered by all the above. **Something new beckons!**

Recovery of WHAT? Childhood? - - *Second* childhood? - - Innocence? - - "Act your Age!"
"Grow up!" Child-like wonder *becomes* looking *ahead* for fulfillment-*becomes* longing, yearning- *becomes* empty. Emptiness is liberating and frees the soul, an obsolete belief system has us thinking emptiness is something to be sad about.

Carefree BEING *becomes* "what will you be when you grow up?"- *becomes* "you must focus"- *becomes* "grow up and act your age" (what the hell is THAT???) - *becomes* "hey, lighten up!"
   HOW CAN I???   Become, become, become! Just BEING seems to resonate with me more than striving to become anything.

★ The Power of IGUAZU ★

12 Noviembre

The 'misadventures' begin. When my companion firmed up our arrangements with the handsome young men at the local travel agency (who spoke no English), the overtones of flirtation created an oversight in the booking of our hotel at Iguazu Falls. Although I had posed questions for my young friend to ask (she speaks fluent Spanish), I could sense she was tiring of my contribution to their conversation and she wanted to take care of it *herself.* Her understandable distraction by the charms of these young men had nobody catch the fact that they booked our hotel on the Brazilian side of the falls. Neither of us had visas to enter that country.

Our 'host' on the bus, a woman who oversaw the entire tour, narrating the sites and assisting the tourists with their needs, tried her hardest to assist us with the problem of no accommodations. We were dog-tired after 24 hours on a bus, and our situation had grim overtones. I was convinced something fabulous would come of it.

I learned in my travel-writing course that mis-adventures make the best stories *after* they have been lived through or endured, and just knew in my heart that this was one of those stories in the making. My frustrated companion didn't have this reference point making her cranky and difficult to reason with.

The choice we had was to stay in a local shanty hotel that was a *negative five-star-awful,* far from the falls, or the 5-star Sheraton *within view of the falls.* My decision to stay at the Sheraton was a choice I emphatically imposed on my more budget-minded companion. This was the first time my friend and I had a disagreement that was unnerving, but when we checked into this luxury establishment, all tensions seemed to dissolve.

Before arriving in the Iguazu area, our bus stopped in the province that was the birthplace of Che Guevara. I only knew this because a photo of him was hanging in the little restaurant, which stated, "It All Began Here". The stop was refreshing despite bad coffee and greasy croissants, but walking around the little street booths where the locals sold their handmade crafts for almost nothing rejuvenated our bus ride wilt. I purchased several rosaries there in Rosario and my camera was actually hot after non-stop extended use, capturing many photos of the locals and this village straight out of a National Geographic magazine.

The next stop was an amethyst mine and we had the privilege to walk through it, being surrounded by giant geodes in their natural habitat. This was an energetic power spot, with mind blowing crystal formations throughout the walls. I lingered there alone after the tour group marched off to another area and stayed in the mine until I was ushered out.

★ HEAVEN ON EARTH ★

<u>14 Noviembre</u>
<u>Sheraton</u>
<u>6:45 A.M.</u>   I G U A Z U

It's too early for coffee-service by 15 minutes.

Sitting in the last slither of shade protecting me from the blast of the rising sun puts a tree between my line of sight and an unobstructed view of the' Devil's Throat', that infamous focal point of intensity and power throughout the entire falls area. I find the name 'Devil's Throat' devastatingly inappropriate for the sacred site before my eyes. Although it's still early morning, the direct sunlight is blinding and the shade is refreshingly cool. The mist from the falls rising high into the sky becomes a dancing cloud still in my view despite the tree, and the mighty roar of the falls in the distance serenade me.

Reverence fills me, as the gift before my eyes is direct from the hand of the Creator. Power, beauty and magnificence are pale words to describe this Divine Artistic Creation with which I am immersed. As witness, I feel wrapped in the blessing.

This chronicle is a gift I offer in gratitude for Divine Providence filling the spirit of all children with inspiration and ecstasy. The love returns to the Source when the children recognize themselves as this. I am this child. We are all one child of Creation.

I feel incredible peace and emptiness, yet fullness simultaneously. I am enraptured in the heart of the Creator. Pen down.

* * *

The worker is handsome with his combed black hair, soulful brown eyes and sweet expression as he softly sings a song. His moves are with focused ease while silently arranging the patio furniture back into place after washing the terrace. Jungle bird sounds strewn about bestow a feeling of total peace within the wild.

I could die here in this moment, content to write while I wait for coffee. I detect it being brewed from the hearty scent reaching me here on the terrace. The aroma of coffee bestows a sweet anticipation of the taste sensation and pleasure to come.

7 A.M. - Ahhh, it's Coffee Time!!

Just photographed my cup of morning coffee here on the terrace, the backdrop being the majestic falls. Need I say more: Contentment-100%. Reset of Mind-100%. Reset of Body-100%. Reset of Spirit-100%. Feeling totally refreshed!!!

Now, to just BE with this cup in my delicious solitude. Pen down.

✴ INTERRUPTION FROM HELL ✴

20 Minutes Later ...

My insides have rumbled halfway through my cup of steaming celestial nectar, and I find myself shitting in El Bano with a force unlike I've ever known. In fact, I almost did not quite make it to le toilette! I had to grab my journal and pen, abandon my heavenly seat, cup of bliss and run full speed to the bathroom. I am writing as I sit here, and shit here, in this tiny cubicle of hell, as I cannot just sit, convulse, shit, convulse some more and allow these miserable colonary explosions to overtake me without chronicling every miserable moment. I can only attribute this as the cleansing part of life's reset button I had intentionally pushed with no idea of the outcome.

One must take great care with what one asks for. Requests are sometimes honored in very accurate yet unexpected ways. **Why can I not stop chronicling everything????** It has always been this way with me.

The memory of my coffee sitting unattended at my table beckoning my sip sweeps over me as my body convulses in yet another round of purgatorial colonic hell.

Only a diehard writer would chronicle a blow-by-blow (literally) account while actually sitting on the toilet experiencing Montezuma's Revenge to this extraordinary degree. I wonder what is the name of that God of Intestinal Hell who reigns in Argentina. Montezuma belongs to Mexico.
Praise to God no one else is in this restroom!

The rest of the day was spent in bed with frequent, rapid excursions to the toilet. We sent out for charcoal medicine to be delivered. My trusty companion went out exploring, but checked in on me frequently. I either slept or watched cartoons, a great way to learn Spanish, curled up in fetal position unable to move. After a dinner of bland white rice, I melted into sleep completely exhausted and emptied of all my old shit.

★ A HEAVENLY ADVENTURE ★

15 Noviembre
5:00 A.M.

Early dawn. Can't see these pages in the darkness, my writing needs no eyes for the pen to scribe. Jungle birds riotous. Stomach restored but still sensitive from yesterday's explosive cleansing. It's almost perfect lighting for a photo foray. A new day is here and I'm occupying a clean, new body. **To just BE here right now in 'today' is a glorious moment!**

The sounds outside beckon me to immerse myself in them. With a delicious sleepiness, I will creep out into the dark purple slice of time between the worlds of night and day with my beloved camera. Today will make up for missing one day of wilderness adventure detoured by the side-trip to hell. I anticipate the sacredness of today's adventure to be multiplied exponentially as it will be experienced from a totally empty vessel, ready and open to walk through the door that has been summoning me. **I believe the door is a portal, and it is here in this hallowed place that the shift will most likely occur.** Mosquitoes will be thick...pen down.

Must   Go   Take   Pictures...

15 Noviembre

Bedtime

Today was the 'awesome' I was looking for. Began with an early hike before the turistas crowded the trails. Many great photos jumped into my camera. Restored to health 100%! We 'ran' the raft ride to the Devil's Throat and around the falls area and indeed, it was *something* to have **done!** My inner adventurer experienced total **orgasmic** pleasure. The drenching from the spray of the raging falls gave my soul complete freedom to emerge from the abyss of my deepest self and hover above life, laughing uproariously. The magnitude of the power released from this water was beyond literal description, as its cascade of sheer force from Creation itself was deafening. That experience was the shift my soul hungered for. Screaming with **total** abandon: "**OTRA, OTRA!**" We yelled until the guide took us back for another round of drenching. The sense of abandon with which I screamed on the absolute top of my lungs for a prolonged period engulfed me and washed my entire cellular matrix with a high pressure blast. A new me was emerging from Iguazu. I felt a true baptism had occurred for the newly born Ave. I am being transformed.

Some time after that sacramental experience we decided to walk the very long pasarelas (catwalks) extending a mile out over the river to the top of the 'Garganta del Diablo' (the gigantic Devil's Throat). Once there, a very large group of pushy tourists intensely challenged my claustrophobia when overlooking the falls. The photography was excellent, the people shockingly rude, and the opportunity to stand so close to this extreme torrential power of nature was altogether unforgettable. My focus to photograph this glorious work of Nature with the angle of sunlight creating multitudes of rainbows overcame the challenge of being out over the falls with far too many people. They were all holding umbrellas and used them to push and poke anyone not in their group out of their way while haggling in a language foreign to this native land and me. They were not friendly, considerate or conscious and wanted the view for themselves only. It was beyond my comprehension that people could display such despicable behavior in the presence of such magnificent power.

This catwalk extends for a mile over the river and out to the top edge of The Devil's Throat. It bridges small islands, which are reminiscent of giant 'stepping stones' along the way. To walk over this expanse of a quiet, serene and easy flowing river to be met with the voluminous power of this deafening, mighty waterfall is to experience another portal to a reality beyond our limited sight and sensory perceptions. I feel myself to be transported to the threshold of a dimension of existence outside our field of human familiarity. I embrace the expansion.

☆ SECRET SWIM & CANDY KISSES ☆

16 Noviembre
Bedtime

This morning was my solo expedition to the falls before the tourist invasion. I left at dawn armed with camera and residual sleepiness. There upon the catwalk, I had the good fortune to befriend a young man who was an eco-tour guide for the Iguazu Wilderness. He spoke some English, I spoke some Spanish and together we became instant friends, kindred adventurers. He explained many things about the area and asked if I would like to go swimming in a secret part of the river accessible only to the guides.

The fire of adventure within me ignited to full flame as we hopped the fence, bushwhacked through dense jungle and arrived at this secret paradise. Vines scratching my legs created a tingling sting. The stinging was a delicious sensation and I felt 'kissed by the jungle'. I disrobed, jumped in and swam about; wrapping my body around rocks while my handsome new friend photographed me with my camera.

I was grateful to have worn my bathing suit, I thought, knowing I would get soaked at the edge of the falls. But when I removed my shorts, much to my surprise, I hadn't worn the suit bottom as I had no idea I'd actually be completely disrobing to swim.

Dressing while half asleep in the darkness, I had no recollection of what I had actually worn. Removing my shorts quickly with the confidence of having worn my full swimsuit, my surprising realization came too late. Looking down, I noticed I was wearing the skimpiest of panties I bought in Paris! It was too humorous a moment to create embarrassing discomfort. "Oops!" was the immediate thought that crossed my mind as I maintained an aire of confidence submerging into the river quickly, hoping he hadn't noticed.

After a brief time he put the camera down, swimming up to me slowly he politely asked if I would accept a shoulder massage. Inhibitions melted into complete bliss during these adventurous moments in the wild, how could I NOT accept? This young man's strong hands kneaded my neck and shoulders with a gentle strength and tenderness that transported me to a world within our world that is glimpsed too seldom and is so fleeting. The water's flow over my body in this river, with the loving touch of this beautiful nature spirit embodying a young Argentine man, was the culmination of the powers of earth, nature, love, man, woman and spirit. There was nothing else.

In those moments, only those moments existed. We stepped into the natural state of *being*. No agendas, no past, no future, no tension, no fear. **Mind dissolved into the bosom of infinity.**

Kisses sweeter than candy with embraces of strength and passion not lust's desperation,
was the gift of Love from That which Created all. I have been shown a portal through which to walk from the realization and acknowledgment of this power; only instead of *walking*, **I danced without touching the ground.**

My guess is that he in fact did notice the mismatched swimsuit components, commenting repeatedly on the beauty he was "gifted to see in the form of this woman". He spoke these words sugar sweet in his heavy Argentine accent –I was moved to the dream-state of another world! Of any encounters of passion or romance to be experienced, this was a most powerful spiritual transformation, as we stood surrounded and immersed in the wilds of these most powerful waters. The potency of the infinite came through us both as we experienced the power of a baptism within the flowing river.

Serenading myself alone to the falls and back, I departed our secret place with a smile on my face and a bounce in my step. No rainbows danced as the late morning light reflected white on the waters, but I had the falls to myself, and the feeling bestowed was an **adventurer's orgasm.** The rainbows were dancing in my heart with the awakening I just experienced submerged in the river with Dani. We were given to each other just for these sacred moments. I stood alone at the edge of the torrential falls between the worlds of life as I knew it, and the other world that has been summoning me safely home as a lighthouse to a ship out at sea.

Upon arrival back from the falls to where Dani was working, he invited me to partake in a raft tour down one of the hidden fingers of the many tributaries going off into the jungle. A few tourists joined us before we could dash away for private boarding, but soon their tour ended and ours continued long enough to enjoy a quiet rafting experience, ducking beneath long, willowy vines and tree limbs hanging over the silent waterway. The light in our mutual gaze was eclipsed only by the sun's blinding reflection in the ripples of the moving waters.

He picked tiny fruits growing from a wild tree and fed me these sweetest of jungle candies. Too soon we had to part, but the smile upon my face and in my heart confirmed an awakening deep and far reaching into the core of my being. The day's remaining activities found me quite buoyant and sparkling. I feel as if I had transcended who I thought I was into a channel of Divine Love and pure awareness, never to be lost again in the illusion of the mundane world. **Another level of my newness has emerged.**

★ SWEET IGUAZU REMINISCENTS ★

17 Noviembre
5:30 AM

One jungle bird screams its exotic call in the pre-dawn world between darkness and light.
Our time in this sacred place will soon end, evoking a tender sadness as I will be leaving a part of myself that belongs here, as here, I have truly been born.

Returning to the grinding city noises raise trepidation as I lay in the silence. Nestling with this fear in this crisp, delicious bed, I enjoy a journey of remembrance of my sweet encounter and private baptism in the river with Dani. All feelings of angst over the long haul to Buenos Aires on the bus and the flight home melt within the embrace of a gift I get to keep forever.

The silence of the forest and sound of waterfalls at my California home will nurture my newness that has emerged from this beautiful country. I couldn't fathom returning to a place that did not have its own wild beauty after being here, and am deeply grateful for my own private wilderness.

After two months in the noisy city, a place I've come to love despite the early morning auditory assaults, thoughts of my sanctuary at home soothe any sadness from my upcoming departure. My freedom in Argentina has provided much needed fun despite the shadowy abyss of adventures deep into the core of who I thought I was. It has been fabulous to walk, ride in cabs and have driving not be an integral part of daily life. A lightness of being has emerged.

Reuniting with my family will be marvelous. Unlike the thrill of the boat ride into the falls and the adventures I've experienced in this beautiful culture, the love of family is a gift of a different color.

The swallows dive into the thick of the falls, dancing in flight through the heavy mist and raging torrents. I stand amazed in the presence of this majestic work of the Creator's play. Feeling a vibratory residue from the ancient sacrifices of virgins that were thrown into these raging torrents, I wondered if it was from the very spot I stood. That was a predominant sense I received standing alone on the catwalk, my receptors fully open after my baptismal ecstasy.

Surrounded by international tourists, I drink in another round of bliss seated on a bench in the open back of an old safari truck. We made our way over dusty, bumpy trails through the jungle to the entry point at the river taking our raft to the wild, raging waters beneath Iguazu's Garganta del Diablo. My **ALIVENESS ignites!** Adventure *is* my soul.

Skimming on the turbulent river, all senses tingling, my mind evaporated. There was nothing outside these moments as I merged into the surroundings, losing all sense of individuality. Nothing mankind conjures up to ingest comes close to this natural high!

Adventure is pure joy. I am gifted to be here.

Rescued a bug from drowning and put it next to the pool. As it recovered, a big lizard quickly ate it. When your time's up, your time *is up!*

I will miss you, Argentina.

Tango, martial arts or belly dancing, I need something to get my body *moving* again- -feel alive with passion for passion's sake. Belly dancing would get me back flowing with my body, martial arts would empower, condition and make me a 50+ year old bad-ass (I like that idea). Tango would be my last choice as I'm not into such physical closeness with American men and having to 'follow' a male at this point in my life even for dancing is not a tasty thought.

Perhaps I will pursue private lessons, learning the dance properly with professionals. I love the passion of tango, but not in a group of beginners who squeeze my hands too tightly, and are incapable of leading. I have no desire to learn to follow someone who cannot lead. Warriors are not successful when following weak leaders, neither are great dancers.

⋆ MY HEART BELONGS TO ARGENTINA ⋆

21 November

My room in this apartment will soon seem like a dream, the city sounds, the fabulous walks, the musical cadence of the Spanish language. Bar Seis Café mornings for endless lattes and fabulous, cheap, incredibly delicious breakfasts, served while sitting on comfortable chairs and couches (our apartment seating consists of only one very uncomfortable chair). Delicious facturas (pastries). Tango. The neighborhoods. Surprisingly, it was wonderful coming home to the noisy city from the wilderness, enjoying our very own apartment.

When I arrive in my homeland I will be between worlds, yet not completely in either. Alone, I'll drink mate (pro: mah'-tay), which may help retain some threads from this world. Working with the hundreds of photographs I've taken, about 3,000 actually will keep the experience fresh and alive.

Cab rides, the powerful Iguazu, the cathedrals, all the inexpensive EVERYTHING. The amazing sushi dinners and too-much sake for less than twenty bucks. Desayuno Americano! **Che's world. . . I love it!** Cobblestone streets. Argentine countryside. The rural provinces and their people. **Ah, the people!** Train rides. The dog walkers. My PIGEONS! *All* the pigeons! Melodies of the caged canaries singing from the upstairs apartments lining the streets of the neighborhood. Palermo. Ah, Palermo! My heart will remain always in this country, this neighborhood! The feral cats of the Botanical Gardens and the Recoleta. Cute cops. Running across the streets to miss oncoming traffic that stops for no one. Grinding bus sounds. Springtime's purple jacaranda trees everywhere. Bottled water from the glacier.

<u>22 Noviembre</u>
<u>5:30 A.M.</u>

I love this world between darkness and the light of a new day.

The tango couple maintains eye contact with a 'deep connection'. I can't seem to attain this with Carlos, my instructor, as the woman who is also my instructor is his wife, and I feel uncomfortable establishing this necessary 'connection' with somebody's husband. It's a very intimate connection from the *heart*. This is not a *concept* from a different culture, but the nuts and bolts of the *essence* of *this* culture so different from mine. We are raised without awareness of such a connection even existing! A connection remotely resembling this in *my* uptight homeland means *sex*, not *connection*.

There are no Starbucks here. No fast paced Americans standing in lines for their fancy coffee drinks 'to-go'. Here, the locals sit in cafes watching the world go by while fully engaged in their coffee, their coffee partner, their newspaper or themselves. I haven't seen anyone eat while walking, driving or doing anything else.

Mealtime is a part of this culture that is savored. Food on the run neither nourishes nor gratifies, a reason my country may have so many unhealthy people.

The ritual of sharing mate (rhymes with latte) here is different from anything North American and a major thread in the tapestry of this culture. People have their thermoses of hot water they can refill at any petrol station. Passing their mate gourd around to their friends in random places, it seems there is no fear of *germs*. **Sharing together, that's their way.**

On the bus arriving from Iguazu back into the city terminal, a group of men in the ghetto shanties seated on crates on what used to be a sidewalk were sharing a smoke and passing the mate. Garbage was everywhere and the buildings were old, demolished industrial sites interspersed with make shift tarp covered 'dwellings'. My camera was glued to my face grabbing 'people shots' from the bus when the men waved to me, smiling and laughing as they gestured for me to join them. What an adventure to have jumped off that bus and immerse myself in the middle of this gang of old timers sharing their mate and a smoke!

I felt compelled to join them and to know them, to sit and converse in their native tongue, as I felt a heart connection with them. This was a 'neighborhood' of homeless people mulling around going about their lives; this group of men, an old woman building a fire on the street corner, rags on her back wearing no shoes, was preparing to cook something. All these people were positively impoverished, dirty and completely bedraggled. The boney stray dogs and skinny cats from starvation and parasitic infestation were too numerous to count.

My heart went out to them all, I was overcome with the desire to help these people.

★ BETWEEN THE WORLDS ★

The journey home was uneventful. There was the combination of a melancholic feeling at leaving this country with which I felt more aligned than my own, and sweet anticipation to see my family and begin life anew. Reunions and the unknown lie ahead. More adventures of a different nature.

27 Noviembre
3:50 A.M.

The freshly stoked fire bathes my home in delicious warmth. It *feels* like the smell of fresh baked bread. Hail remains frozen in patches everywhere from yesterday's pounding. Hail indeed **pounds**.

I left behind a climate heating up to the steamy South American summer, *beaming down* into the frosty beginnings of a northern California winter. Air travel seems to have a similar molecular effect as being beamed from a starship down into a different world. The realignment we call jet lag is the body's reaction to moving unnaturally fast at unnaturally high altitudes. Our molecular structure has not industrialized with the times. We are glorified cavemen.

Unpacking luggage carries me back to Argentina as I integrate back into my California life. I am enjoying this interval of time between the three worlds of my life before, during and now after this odyssey.

As I look at the photo cards of Señor Guevara, I feel the connection reawaken that initially stirred in Argentina. A slight yearning stirs, and I enjoy the memory of those dreams that awakened my heart and soul with him. We may have loved in another time and love each other still, time and space may be irrelevant between dimensions, between love. Anything is possible. The thought of him emanates warmth that soothes my rough edges with a barely discernable yearning that is tender and sweet. I slip back into the bliss from that dream which has a profound and lasting effect. **I am transported to a place I cannot herein describe.**

* * *

I feel complete love and acceptance of myself *AS IS*. Healed of wanting to 'be more'? Healed of the restlessness of not enjoying life in its present moment by striving under my own psychological whip *TO DO MORE?* **We shall see.**

Anyone I speak with says they hear a *difference* in my voice. Will this healing stay with me? **We shall indeed see.**

I keep thinking of all those poor people in the country that feels like my *real* home. I am charged with the drive to go back there and help those people. The memories of their images are burned into my psyche, and I vow that in this lifetime, **I will go back and give something of myself to make a positive difference in as many lives as I can.**

Listening to the innate wisdom that has guided me seems to have served a divine purpose. There is a light burning inside me illuminating a dance I've not felt before. **I am different.**

★ INSPIRATION FOLLOWS EMERGENCY ★

1 December

Tonight my grandbaby underwent an emergency appendectomy. Exhaustion overtakes as I write this, home from hospital long enough for a quick shower to refresh, enabling further service to my daughter and grandbaby. The anguish in witnessing a child so small enduring extreme pain and heavy medication is beyond verbal description. As she is wheeled off to surgery we are in a state I'm unable to describe, without time to sit, no time to journal and no energy to find the words.

3 December

These days in hospital leave no time to think of anything but getting baby Emma through this. Watching her in such pain as nurses move her to initiate walking is **intense**. My tiny, precious Emma is hooked up to an IV administering *morphine* before she is roused for the painful first steps required to engage the healing process. She cries out, tears streaming from the pain, "I will **try**, Mommy, I will **try**." There's an unraveling beneath our encouraging words and smiling faces that serve to encourage her. I embrace those parents who must helplessly witness their child's suffering from serious injury or illness, and am thankful to be home, not learning of this emergency from Argentina! This has taken us all outside ourselves, outside the routine of life's tasks. In a holding pattern, we are placed in the blatant spotlight of only these moments. **There is nothing else.**

8 December
5:05 A.M.

Prompted by a 'nudge' from Spirit, I got up from the comfort of my cozy, warm bed and went down to the creek. Reluctantly, I dressed, and forfeiting the pleasure of morning tea, walked down the hill. There I was filled with the presence of Divine Providence, imparted with a loud, clear message:

"Make this place *work* for you, my little one."

Filled with Spirit, I feel inspiration, clarity and confidence when hearing these words:

"Clear the island, expand creek area by removing all brambles. Healing sessions more potent when held in space by running water. Having this land a place to facilitate human healing will heal land from abuse **it** has endured. Erect platform beside creek for sessions, meditations."

This 'received' information reveals what appears like a direction my life is to take. Establish a place of healing for people to be surrounded by the serene beauty of this land with the creek that runs through it. Will I become a facilitator for the healing of others, my services sought as an actual healer, or will my land be the place I develop as an intimate retreat for people to come experience their own healing?

This detail is not clear although Spirit gave me this message clearly at the water's edge. I will commence clearing the brambles.

Little Emma is home, having to maintain calmness, proving as difficult as keeping a puppy still. We are thankful her hospital stay is over and she is recovering.

"The Pigeon Chronicles" is my priority to complete. Researching children's books in the library and pigeons online have my inspiration flowing. I am learning much about these birds and how to assemble a story line. I now must consider which age group this story will best serve. Do I include the chick that died and have the story assist children in learning that death and grief are part of life? To not fear death, but view it as a natural occurrence? To use the pigeon's real life story to teach how to grieve a loss and still be ok? Do I leave out the death of the chick altogether and write that happily ever after theme so overdone in children's tales? This last consideration does not feel aligned with the purpose to best serve.

I want this book to be *more* than just another narrative on the fluff of life that doesn't matter. This story will break the cycle that entertains without serving the child's true nature. The direction this story takes will develop a life of it's own. I am ready for guidance.

I learned online that parent pigeons frequently let the weakest of their two chicks die by withholding food as a natural form of controlling population, allowing only the strongest to survive. It's the theme in the world of animals, like it or not. I was witness to the grief of the stronger of the two chicks and how profound yet brief that process was for it. It did learn to fly from its parental nest. Imagine the multitudes of pigeons on the planet if the parent birds let both chicks live? The perfection of the forces of nature does not require human understanding. Accepting what is, however, will allow us joy and a sense of ease as we pass through the journey of the human experience.

So much to consider in the creation of a book!

10 Diciembre
Sunday Morning

I again find myself filled with Spirit this morning as water pours down from the sky. Any slice of wakefulness in the night finds me calling spirit as a child calls for its parent. Upon waking, I acknowledge the day to be a classroom of learning. I call forth Divine Providence to be the driver of this vehicle called my life. Surrendering the reins to Creator, I feel relaxed at inviting Infinity to 'run the show'. To frequently summon Spirit aloud is one of the advantages of living completely alone; a partner or dog would look at me with curiosity, questioning my sanity at these verbal evocations. **I am totally free!**

Spirit's actual presence invokes enthusiasm to just BE, as it bestows energy, inspiration, and knows no fear. **I find this union actually *dissolves* fear.**

＊ CHE BECKONS ＊

11 Deciembre

In my earliest hours laying half awake embraced by darkness, I tune my day to be aligned with 'That Which Created me' in my thought, action, intent, emotion, movement, goals and attitude. This is the most potent time of day, the raining has ceased, stillness rules, and in my woodstove the fire is a pile of silent embers. There is an occasional drip from saturated trees hanging over my bedroom yurt. Such a preferred sound to that of the grinding buses and traffic in Buenos Aires.

(Note: the 'yurt' is a round structure with canvas material over lattice framework. It comes as a kit assembled free standing in retreat sites or for wilderness lodging. Mine was erected and attached to the cabin serving as my bedroom. Yurts originated in ancient times, housing nomadic tribes on the Mongolian steppes and are still used by these people, layering animal skins over the lattice frame)

I find myself compelled to read about the dead revolutionary. "Whatever *for?*" Why do I *care?* For a reason obscured from familiar frames of reference, I not only *care* to know, but find I **need** to know and purchased a book. In retrospect, I assumed my thoughts and connection so strong with Señor Guevara in Argentina came alive within me because I was *in 'his native country'*.

In those moments during that time his presence overtook me, there were no thoughts of the 'future', therefore didn't consider this prevailing when I came home. Hadn't *thought* about the homecoming while immersed in adventure and reinvention on the beloved continent I've left behind. Argentina still beckons my heart and soul.

I was connected with him at *that* time and enjoyed immensely the lingering intensity of his presence, having no thoughts of a future containing those moments. It was just *what it was then*: an awakening of my *own* love and passionate essence, opening further my mind, heart and spirit. The opening of this portal allowed me a glimpse through the veil that diffuses human awareness from the dimension of Source Energy ... where the spiritual essence resides of who *was* the man, Ernesto Che Guevara.

This seemed a logical explanation of the energy behind those haunting pictures and dreams, and I accepted my sanity as intact, my own rhythm just beating to a different drum.

I have plans of my *own* here, *and this was not part of that picture!* (Che *does not remotely resemble a pigeon!*) Now I find those birds to be lovely creatures, whereas before Argentina, they stirred no interest or emotion.

His energy has popped back into my life after I've settled into my surroundings with the *new me.* With Emma's medical emergency, I'd forgotten about that persistent, pesky connection with the dead guy. Perhaps the energetic resonance of this person is *part* of me and I was unaware of this aspect of myself. We shall see!

I just *found MYSELF* in Argentina, and have fallen in love with *ME!* I have this inspired project to become one with, and with great joy anticipate creating this book from the photographs and notes taken during my study. This will be a story of nature and growth, to inspire others, as I am inspired. My task will involve matching pictures with story. I'm excited about this project, utilizing my art and writing skills. *I have plenty to do without nurturing some bizarre curiosity over Ernesto Che Guevara.*

His journal from the days of his adventure in THE MOTORCYCLE DIARIES express a similar sentiment in writing style as I *feel*. **I'm detecting a feeling within me that resonates with the essential source being now in non-physical, that was the man in that infamous life.**

Something is opening up in me as I read his journal. On some levels he seems a kindred spirit: a romantic, adventurer and chronicler, in search of his place in the world. We are both captivated by indigenous ruins, share the love of photography and thirst for travel. We are both restless spirits with an asthmatic condition. (His severe, mine slight) Many people no doubt have a similar combination of traits, *surely*. Yet I cannot help but notice so many similarities between us. **I wonder if he wrote poetry or sang tango.**

I'm sure millions of people had the same feeling about him I am now experiencing. It's no doubt the same phenomenon as the connection of the masses and how they personally related to Princess Diana. I'm sure this is something that happens to people all the time when they visit Argentina. It's probably an everyday occurrence.

12 Diciembre

Che. I went to Argentina and was 'formally introduced to him'. Now, I feel an awakened love with him as if he was alive and we actually met. Though I actually *experience* this, I honestly find it quite weird at the same time. Have I gone over the deep end? **Che**. He has charged into the quiet solitude of the sanctuary of my home and has made his presence quite noticeable. Is my imagination just longing for companionship? **Maybe I *should* get a puppy.**

It's raining, not too cold, and beautifully serene.
The photo of Che on his book, Motorcycle Diaries, is the face that I experience an intense yet eerie attraction to. The book compels me to pick it up and look at it. ***Compelled by a book???*** This is too bloody weird for even *me*, **ok?** Something about this not only doesn't feel wrong, but actually feels RIGHT. The resonance is palatable. My logical mind labels it weird, my essential nature and spirit find this awakening completely "in order" and nothing about it feels like I'm losing my mind, but experiencing an opening within my heart and soul. **I hear a calling and FEEL it as well.**

I feel such an affinity with that image, that in the moments those eyes catch mine and rivet me to them, my heart races and I experience the same sensations as seeing a love that is alive, new and on fire. I *actually remember* those long past feelings with *mortal* men. I keep the book out of sight, but there is a magnetic pull between it and myself and it **calls** to me. **What the hell???!**

Remembering the summer before going to Argentina and experiencing a prolonged, intense desire to get a motorcycle and take a road trip around an entire country, not necessarily mine, was abstract. I had wondered what was up with this out-of-character motorcycle fantasy. I even asked my neighbor to show me how to ride his. *A motorcycle???*

I am feeling the pull to utilize my open mind, love of adventure and creative gifts to uplift and inspire people to follow their dreams and don't settle for fulfilling mundane societal impositions.

13 Diciembre

I love my cozy solitude. I love living close enough to my daughter so little Emma can walk over and knock on my door. I get to have the best relationships with both daughters. They have turned into glorious, wholesome women with good family and spiritual values. They are visual confection with their outer beauty and inner light. I am one of the most fortunate humans on the face of the entire earth right now, in this very moment. **Money cannot buy the gifts I have.**

Life gets *fabulous* after 50, sounds cliché, who *cares*. Survived multiple heartbreaks, now I'm filled with Source Energy, ("God") who is my companion, roommate, partner and protector. I experience serenity more often and for longer periods than those fleeting glimpses of it in my past. It's amazing how deep and wide the fingers of ego-based fears reach and wrap around every fiber of one's being, flowing on mind currents, basically taking over a life. When uprooting ego, it fights to survive, but my desire for a joyful life is stronger and wins the battle almost every time! When I choose to not dwell on that which is painful, I become an empowered master over the monkeys of my mind that used to run me over.

The attacks become harder to detect and requires CONSTANT vigilance to maintain Spirit realization as ego sneaks about and pounces unexpectedly. Little bastard!

Will it always be waiting in the wings easing in a disturbing judgment of myself or someone else? Will it always be hovering in the shadows trying to make me feel the slightest unsure feeling like I don't belong or should be doing something else? Will it dampen my spirit with self-criticizing judgments that I'm not doing enough?

I imagine it waits in the shadows of my mind ready to pounce, and will most probably take shots at me as the inner critic with that eternal whip. It is my choice to not feed this dragon.

Is this bizarre burning connection of love with Che an ego tactic? It matters not if he's dead, as death is as illusory as life, and his spirit and I connect and this love needs nothing else. It just IS. Even *thinking and writing* this, feels *way* outside the box of my usual thinking of even the most unusual thoughts I've sometimes had!

This expansion of my essence is very uncomfortable yet to pretend it's not happening is more uncomfortable. The idea of this being mental illness doesn't resonate with me at all.

★ CHE SPEAKS ★

14 Diciembre

So how is it I find this connection with Che Guevara growing deeper even after I leave his continent and find my own direction?

True, we have things in common. I feel an affinity of sorts with his 'spirit', yet in reality, there are many people who share these interests with whom I share no alignment or energetic connection. To look upon that one photo, our eyes meet and sensations run through my core that I find *unnerving*. This is a picture of the young Ernesto, not the movie star photos of the famous revolutionary.

"He's DEAD", I tell myself. "Handsome, yes he was, so what, he's dead."

"Death does not matter."

I 'hear' these faint but very clear words deep within my psyche.

"Death is a word humans call a transition they do not understand."

These 'words' do not come from my own thoughts; they are being 'received'.

It is not the first time in my life I have 'received' wisdom, and after 50 years on the planet, I know the difference between my OWN thoughts and 'received information'. Received information is not 'heard' by our ears, is not in the form of 'voices' in one's head, and is without gender.

The essence of Guevara and I seem to be aligned in some unexplainable way. But there are many souls who experience alignment - **so?** I am not under the influence of alcohol, drugs, herbs or medications, nor am I feeling lonely and creating this due to an overactive imagination or the desire to have a partner. I tell myself this and I question, *'what the hell???'*

Something, clearly, is awakened within me when he randomly invades my headspace no matter what else I'm doing. It's wild, strange and refreshing all at the same time. I like it.

★ MY INVISIBLE ROOMMATE ★
WHO NEEDS A PUPPY!

21 Diciembre

The winter solstice stealing autumn heralds in a blustery season, and holidays are upon us. Less introspection and trying to figure things out, more drawing of pigeons and taking long walks.

I need a break from this Che connection that continues no matter how crazy I think it is and ignore it. I'm very busy with my book's preliminary work, no time for ghostly shenanigans. I don't mind reading his books for historical value although there's no telling what the facts really were.

3 January
1:00 A.M.

As I read "Death of a Revolutionary", I am hosting a fight against asthma and bronchitis. My inhalers are expired and breathing is difficult.

Che's *presence* has once again been unnerving. Reading in this book tonight and learning how he was too headstrong to clearly see the odds against him with how clear the signs were, I felt a wave of disgust over his judgment and actions. Upon feeling his chosen path *stupid for how intelligent he allegedly was*, and how he *should have chosen a life being a father to his children*, an immediate menacing sensation filled my peaceful cabin. **Dude!**

I felt an intense sensation resembling imminent danger to my person, causing me to check the locks on my doors and windows.

I actually *feel* him rearing up with intense anger against **me**, so close as to be *in my face*, then pacing around enraged. The extremely strong and unexpected presence outside myself is *totally creeping me out*. It's the same vibe and fright I experienced living in a Texas rental house decades ago haunted by a spirit whose person was murdered there before we moved in (we didn't know this when we rented it). I literally ran out of that house when the energy was as menacing as this feels now. I am closing this book, turning off the light and curling up under my covers.

* * *

I can still feel his rage, with a "knowing" that it is from my judgment of his actions in Bolivia. So strong it is, that I turned the light back on to write this down. I'll attempt darkness and sleep, but this energy *outside* of myself has me fully awake at 1:11 a.m. I finally say out loud, "Okay, okay, I'm **sorry**, I wasn't *there*, I'll try to not judge you. **Just back off okay?**"

I am immediately filled with the words:

"I **had** no place to go except to my death, the life of Che had run its course."

Don't know how easy sleep will come after *this!*

4 January

Rain. Lovely i'tis. Bestows peace. Warm cabin. Dark outside. I clearly feel *the presence* with me. Imagination? Dead revolutionaries are safe to love?

As I write that, I hear the instantaneous and emphatic,
"I'm not dead."

Illustrating the 'chronicles' brings me peace. When old thought forms of fear and limitation threaten, I drown it out with the ever-present invitational 'call' for Spirit to illuminate my life. Spirit doesn't take this as an *open invitation*, I have to call on a regular basis.

Dawn's light is brightening the dark windows, and the outline of the trees appear black against a colorless sky. How quickly the sky brightens indicates the swiftness of time passing. How many souls can I awaken to their divinity through my own awakening? Everything I do will serve that purpose. I am an uplifter, this I know for sure.

My mind flashes back to a moment when I was a toddler, yet unable to actually speak. I recall fully formed thoughts and clearly recall even the *tone* of one thought in particular while standing in front of the bathtub in our modest bathroom: I looked down at my tiny naked baby body and remember exclaiming to myself in wonder and amazement, **"Wow, I'm a white woman in America!"**

This memory, although I've always had it, seems to be 'highlighted' right now, indicating a recollection trying to break through. My Latin American journey sparked it. As I write this, Che's presence is all around me. We are chroniclers. My flow here stops as his energy *is in my brain- - -* embraced in a delicious loving light, I cannot move.

* * *

... a bit later ...

I've asked for a 'sign', positive in its essence that this is *not* my imagination. (I am *still* very skeptical) That request was yesterday. When I sit here today and repeat my request aloud for a morning direction in this regard, I 'get the message' to brew a cup of mate and go down to the creek. Is this mate suggestion 'the sign'?

The water boils, sending up a rolling steam. Early light illuminates the world out of sleep. Cloud cover and rain have the dark gray light diffused, yet everywhere. I'm hungry.

5 January

Asthma tightens my chest. No inhaler. When I learned what *Che* endured with this illness, mine pales by comparison. Being claustrophobic, any restriction of breath creates anxiety.

I'm on a quest to learn what the hell is happening here.

I am feeling unsettled with this **frequent** 'presence', yet curiosity overrules ignoring it at this point. Ignoring it doesn't seem to work anyway. I don't evoke it, but am open to observing whatever *this is*. **I am not allowing my mind to close on this blatant shift indicative that something is *definitely* going on.**

The only *remote* description of this is that it feels like a being from some other dimension is <u>*right in my face*</u>. It might be invisible to the five senses and my logical mind, but I FEEL the pressure and intensity of it in my *own* energy field. Sometimes it scares the hell out of me, but it seems like it's really trying to get my attention. Today I can focus on the island being cleared of brambles by men I hired for completion of this enormous job. I keep reminding myself this fear is the ego that wants everything in logical, predictable order.

★ CHE'S EVICTION ★

6 January

Finally, my curiosity gives way to literally **kicking it out of my life.** I prayed out loud the way we prayed in the Baptist church living in Texas decades ago: "In the Name of the Lord Jesus Christ, I rebuke you from my life!!!" It's worth a try, why ever not? **And now the presence should be gone.**

Now my psyche can be fully restored and I can get on with my life. Chalk it up to a vivid imagination, temporary infatuation with a Hollywood face, a crush on the image of a dead revolutionary, temporary insanity---sounds good. And now I know I will not be deemed insane for thinking I hear (and am inhabited by) *dead people.*

Am I buying into what I fear others will think of me and giving in to THEIR fears by taking them on myself, thereby denying something happening here that is in perfect resonance for my own expansion? In my heart, I KNOW I'm not what is deemed 'crazy' by the masses of limited mind.

The fire's dancing and I'm cozy in my robe under the covers. Although my shoulder hurts, it diminishes not the delicious state of squeaky clean after my long shower and nesting in crisp, clean linens. **The nest I call my bed is my personal slice of heaven.**

The island looked magnificent yesterday with crunchy patches of residual hail scattered about the land right up to the thinly iced edges of the creek. The frostiness of it all was crisp and refreshing.

How many people get to watch their island be cleared of invasive, thorny brambles to expose a mini paradise? **I am so blessed.**

This gift evokes deep appreciation. My psyche is relieved of Che. I release whatever/whoever this character is/was. Realigning my attention back to the Divine Creative Force and my life's purpose.

★ CHE'S RETURN ★

7 January

Frosty, freezing and crunchy out there. Two wood piles lay beneath new camo tarps- -feels good, that. I can't stand bright blue tarps.

I love my headspace now compared to before leaving for Argentina, but don't want to stagnate *here* either. *Continued* growth is key. Writing in this moment, I'm 'nudged' to consider my ability to facilitate healing sessions. **I sense amazing events to unfold before me.**

Che once again summons my attention when I'm doing other things. Yesterday at work, changing linens in the treatment room between clients, his presence enveloped me *so* strongly I could not move for a short lapse of time. As I'm writing this, his presence is palatable. There's been a shift and now I am filled with actual *love* for this energy, like he's in my life as 'someone' I know and have known. I'm given a reminder to record my "Message" song and then get it onto a rebel radio station. I had forgotten I'd even written this song so long ago. The name I am to assume has come through in a flash while embraced in this wave of euphoric love: Ave, (pro: Ah'-vay), as in Ave Maria.

Don't know how it will be my identifying endorsement yet, but when I scribe 'A-v-e' over and over developing a feel for it, the connected letters look like C-H-E. I didn't realize this while engaged in the exercise, but afterward when studying signature possibilities this similarity presented itself. **Why does this *not* surprise me?**

"If you love something, let it go, if it returns..." I know that quote well. I let this presence go totally. It has returned, this time with a calm, loving vibration. I sense it to truly be in perfect accordance with my current life experience. My mind is open, my heart is open, I live out in nature away from societal distractions, therefore, I feel RIPE for this mystical, expansive experience. If anyone thinks I'm crazy, it is their limited thinking, and I cannot allow my fear of their opinion to influence something currently unexplainable that feels sacred and POWERFUL.

8 January
Grand Hyatt, San Francisco

My employer and I are in The City for a seminar. We left class early, hitting the sunny streets of Union Square. Stopping to admire much and buying nothing, we found ourselves in my favorite place to accidentally spend *a lot* of money...a gigantic bookstore! In the sale section, one need not spend much to carry out a very heavy bag or two. **There are *so many* books in the world!** It bestows awe, as does the library. Only differences being the endless selection of books are all clean, new, and not free.

The bookstore is a place for me to forget myself and simply be enlivened. My senses fully awakened at the endless possibilities of countless worlds waiting to be explored between the colorful covers. One can judge a book by its cover or not, but there are certainly some enticing book covers out there. I could *LIVE* in a bookstore!

I enjoy walking around all the sections, not just those serving personal interests, to see which books jump out at me. There are just *so many* books one must begin *somewhere* (the sale section is both my first *and* last stop on the route).

I wasn't even *thinking* about him. In all my bookstore wanderings, I've never run into a shelf containing these books; but I found myself standing before two shelves of books by and about Che Guevara. In my amused state of **'I can't escape him!'** I stared at all these books holding my mind at an open blank. **I was amused at this point. This was ostentatiously uncanny.**

His Bolivian Diary was the first book to jump. I took it and hightailed straight to the sale section, resisting the stronger urge to peruse the shelves in detail, restraint being a virtue at times.

19 January

Working the Pigeon Chronicles, I've completed five illustrations. I cherish this intensely focused work, my oneness with the creative dimension. It distracts me from 'my invisible friend', as I've humorously and affectionately come to call him.

20 January
5:45 A.M.

Darkness with fire dancing in the woodstove is downright sensual. The flames lick the wood. Switching on the lamp to write disrupts that visual bliss, but scribing in the world between slumber and consciousness is the best time to capture with my pen.

The presence seems to be guiding me and feeling it always, I never feel alone here anymore. In my solitary moments, he is ever present. I wonder if my work as an esthetician's assistant, an occupation that could be deemed a frivolous service, unnecessary and 'bourgeois', repulses my 'revolutionary companion'. The immediate response I receive is,

"none of that makes any difference".

A form of revolution has always been alive in my life and spirit. The Ego is the force to subdue, and belief systems in need of the overthrow. This is the dictator to be ousted from power. My Divine Nature **will** outshine the weeds of darkness cultivated in the soul that has taken root and caused suffering in so many ways. **My own Divine Nature is ready to blossom and be the ruler seated upon the throne of my mind, my life.**

The Capitalists and Imperialists that were the sworn enemy to be destroyed by my ghost in his last incarnation are but the outward manifestation of ego based fear we each carry within our own selves. The struggle with the human condition is only the exterior representation of the conflict within each of us. We have the choice between ego-fear and separation, *OR* awareness with full use of our Divine Nature and self-empowerment. We forget about this option, and become our own oppressors when we choose the fear-based reaction to life's events *out of habit*. We steal from ourselves our own power and view ourselves as 'victims'. The wars governments wage with each other are reflections of the collective consciousness that hold our own individual conflicted nature. Divine essence or limiting belief systems – it's our choice which to embrace.

Now with my daughters grown and I'm not tied into a romance or the yearning for one, I have no distractions, and my authentic purpose for coming to earth can reveal itself fully. What a delicious thought! I've had glimpses throughout my life, but could not devote the time to develop and nurture it as I can now. It has the space to *come to me* and I'm in the space to *receive it*. Without the demands or responsibilities of growing children, a pet or partner, I beam my focus and intent on the purpose of my life.

The sense that has been with me since being a tiny child is that before this life, my existence was without form or density, residing in a realm unencumbered from human limitations.

Walking and use of an automobile seemed cumbersome and backward to my child's mind. The sky seemed more my domain than the earth and I found myself constantly in trouble at school for staring skyward out the window rather than focusing on the lessons. Pertaining to human communication, the spoken word so frequently misunderstood by listener and difficult to express by speaker, seemed vestigial. The sounds of other languages surpass my own in beauty. Why can we not communicate by transferring clear thought to the receiving device in the brain, transcending the language barrier? Why this mechanism is unavailable here has always escaped me! Maybe it's a condition of life on this seemingly primitive dimension.

The marriage I knew I'd have in my 50's is with Spirit. I am *truly* in love with That Which Created All'. I commit to growing within Source as I cannot fathom It's wholeness. Anyone who comes into my life intimately must support my commitment to knowing and developing my divine nature, and currently I have neither desire nor yearning to meet or entertain a mortal companion.

The missionaries recruiting indigenous tribes so long ago may have gone awry due to their judgment, ego-fear and superiority blindness. The original intent may have been noble, but how the mission carried out was corrupted by diseased human minds steeped in their own sense of self-importance, greed and righteousness. A poor representation for the Divine! That same situation still exists; history doesn't repeat itself, it simply continues.

The true temple is our heart, and the creative power of the mind is the choice for ego thought form habits or Divine awareness. Our lives are but vignettes illustrating that choice played out over and over and over.

The personification of this struggle seems represented in my ghost's past incarnation. Representatives carrying truth can have a rough time of it on this planet as a misguided person could act out the insanity of fear. Or one can be judged and shunned by family, friends and/or society.

Many people recoil from truth and may even shoot or torture the messenger. It seems the masses love bullshit as if it were a delicacy to be savored. Not everyone with awareness of basic truth is nice either, and those that use it against others for personal gain pose great danger.

Truth is a funny thing...some 'true stories' aren't necessarily about truth, and all stories about truth aren't necessarily true. This story is about my own personal journey with a truth that I find hard to believe, but reveals itself to be true despite my doubts and fears. My doubts and fears are really my logical ego mind resisting the expansion this experience is giving me in amazing love, color and vibratory essence. It blows my mind beautifully!

This is the sort of experience you read about others having!

<u>25 January</u>
<u>12:40 A.M.</u>

Forty minutes into morning and it's writing time!

Ave.   Spiritual Revolutionary.
          -must stay underground with all this
          -don't change jobs, stay low key
          -consider the book with Neal regarding
            our spiritual awakening decades ago
          -pigeons- - include dead chick in story
          -go down to creek more often
          -don't go to Cuba
          -be quiet about *the presence*

          -study French/Spanish/Tango
          -market photographs/writing
            /artwork- - this
           will provide ample support
          -feel your healing gifts awakening

I retire to bed with my mind transported back to that
mystical experience between Neal and I decades ago that
joined us as *friends for life*. Neither he nor I could explain
the experience in terms anyone could understand, especially
significant others involved over the years. He has recently
suggested we consider writing a book about it, and the idea
of collaborating with him on a project is attractive. His idea
has re-awakened that experience of our youth, an event that
molded our psyches and lives. Full as that event was to us
personally, I am unsure whether the story could occupy an
entire book.

★ ARAVAIPA AWAKENING ★

<u>26 January</u>
<u>1 A.M.</u>

We hiked deep into the wilderness of the canyon, surrounded by towering walls of majestic rock formations, evoking utter amazement and the wonder of small children at Disneyland. We were speechless.

THE STORY OF NEAL AND I, HIKING BUDDIES FOR DECADES. IN OUR FRIENDSHIP'S BEGINNING, WE WERE AWAKENED SIMULTANEOUSLY AND COMPLETELY TO THE AWARENESS OF BEING TWIN SOULS FORMED TOGETHER IN ANOTHER DIMENSIONAL WOMB. ALL DIMENSIONS WERE AWARE OF THE INTERCONNECTEDNESS BETWEEN EACH. THERE WAS NO SEPARATION. THIS WAS THE NATURAL STATE OF INFINITY OF WHICH WE ARE ALL INCLUDED AND ACTUALLY CREATED TO EXPERIENCE.
WE HAVE THE EQUIPMENT!

THIS UNION IN ARAVAIPA CANYON BACK IN OUR TWENTIES ALWAYS HELD THE MYSTERY OF SOMETHING NOT FULLY UNDERSTOOD, HARD TO FIND WORDS TO DESCRIBE, AND NEVER OCCURRING AGAIN.

I FIND AFTER THE AWAKENING WITH CHE FROM THIS OTHER DIMENSION, THE ARAVAIPA MYSTERY HAS HAD LIGHT SHED UPON IT, RENDERING A DEEPER UNDERSTANDING.

THIS EXPERIENCE SO LONG AGO WAS THE INITIAL CRACK IN THE SHELL OF THE EGO MIND OF HUMAN NATURE.

ALL THE PROGRAMMING WE RECEIVED UPON ENTRY INTO THIS LIFE SPILLED OUT IN AN INSTANT, REATTUNING US WITH THE ESSENCE WE NEVER REALLY LOST, BUT THOUGHT WE DID BECAUSE WE WERE TAUGHT TO FORGET SINCE THE ONSET OF OUR BIRTH.

WE WERE SUBMERGED WITHIN THE OCEAN OF CREATION BLENDING
AS TWO DROPLETS OF WATER. COMPLETELY IMMERSED IN OUR OWN
DIVINE NATURE, OUR BLENDING ENERGY FIELDS BESTOWED
RAPTURE UPON US BOTH, ENGULFING EVERY CELL OF OUR BEING
AND CONNECTING US WITH THAT WHICH CREATED ALL.

FREE FROM ANY OTHER HUMAN, SURROUNDED BY THE NATURE-AL
FORCES, MINDS WERE OPENED BY THE FORCE OF NATURE WITH
WHICH WE WERE IMMMERSED. WE WERE WITHIN THE BOSOM OF
TOTAL, REMOTE WILDERNESS, DIVINE NATURE.

TOGETHER WE HAD NO PRE-CONCEPTIONS OF HOW WE 'SHOULD BE'
AS MALE/FEMALE, WHITE AMERICANS, TOTALLY FREE FROM
SOCIETAL IMPOSITIONS. THIS LIBERATION INCITED TOTAL
JOYOUSNESS RESULTING IN UPROARIOUS LAUGHTER, RELEASING
ENDORPHINS FEEDING THE JOYFUL BLISS. HENCE, AN EXTENDED
DANCE WITH OUR ANGELIC ESSENCE.

WE DIDN'T *DANCE*   WE BECAME THE DANCE.
WE DIDN'T *FEEL* THE BLISS   WE *WERE* THE BLISS.
WE DIDN'T *EXPERIENCE* JOYOUSNESS   WE *BECAME* JOY.

TOTAL TRANSCENDENCE OF HUMANNESS TO THE IMMORTAL PLANES
OF DIVINITY,
    WHICH IS THE NATURAL STATE OF EXISTENCE.

        LIFE OUTSIDE THE DREAM.
WE BROKE THROUGH THE DREAM BARRIER WHICH IS THE HUMAN-
INVENTED CHAOTIC STATE OF RESTLESS MIND,
    INSATIABLE YEARNING.

        AT-ONE-MENT
TOTAL GUILTLESSNESS. RADIANT MESSAGE OF
        'GOD'S' LOVE.
    AWAKENING IN HEAVEN. SHINING. INNOCENCE.
                    PURITY.

THE WORLD OF SEPARATION SLIPPED AWAY AND FULL
COMMUNICATION WAS RESTORED BETWEEN THE CREATOR AND THE
CREATED.

   NEAL & I. ONE CREATION IN TWO BODIES.

TOTAL RELEASE FROM
   OUR PERSONAL   SEPARATE   IDENTITIES.

ETERNAL GLORY OF CREATION FILLED US BOTH AND WE WERE OF
ONE MIND.

   NO CONFLICT OF ANY KIND.
      L I M I T L E S S N E S S

WE WERE RESTORED TO THE ORIGINAL STATE OF
      MERGENCE WITH ETERNAL, LIMITLESS, GLORIOUS
            LIGHT AND RAW
         UNFILTERED CREATION.

      (COMMONLY CALLED "GOD")

TOTAL SAFETY. PERFECT PEACE.
THE CIRCLE OF ATONEMENT HAS NO END.

(YET WE MUST "GO BACK" TO OUR SEPARATE LIVES,
COMMONLY CALLED OUR "REAL LIVES")-BUT WHICH LIFE IS REAL?

JOY - - UNIFYING ATTRIBUTE WITHIN THE EMBRACE
            OF THE CREATOR
      LOVE   UNION   HOLINESS
            RESURRECTION
         THE SYMBOL OF THE RELEASE

      REIGN OF LOVE - - CIRCLE OF PURITY

WE WERE RESTORED, AND ABLE TO RECOGNIZE OUR
            ORIGINAL STATE.

THE SEPARATENESS OF HEAVEN AND EARTH
DISSOLVED

A HIGHLY PERSONAL EXPERIENCE OF REVELATION.

THIS IS A DRAMATIC DISCLOSURE.

TOTAL ABANDONMENT OF EGO-BASED
THOUGHTS/PATTERNS/PROGRAMS

COMPLETELY FILLED WITH SPIRIT

NO FEAR BECAUSE THE SOURCE OF FEAR WAS EVAPORATED,
NON-EXISTENT.
THE STATE OF GRACE RESTORED
NO PERCEPTION OF SELF - PERCEPTION UPROOTED.

★ I'M FIFTY-SOMETHING-YIKES! ★

<u>3 Febrero</u>

Morning tea ritual before the earning of daily bread duty is good for the soul. Reflection time, email time, morning pages time, empty mind time-many choices. **Enjoyed my birthday yesterday.**

Governments inflicting death upon revolutionaries or even its own people can thwart the revoluccion! The *SPIRIT* of the revoluccion cannot be killed, as the human spirit cannot be annihilated. Killed yes. Enslaved yes. Made hopeless, you bet. (<:Note: the above words came as my own expression, later to read in one of Che's diaries this sentiment similarly expressed:>) The revolution is to continue, but on the SPIRITUAL LEVEL. Forget politics- - it is a bad platform with which to become involved, too much danger and conspiracy. Nothing is safe for those in that arena. I am a *spiritual* revolutionary, bringing as many humans as possible in touch with their Divine nature by lighting the way with my own life experience. My service is being a flashlight of sorts, through books, music, art and life. No preaching. Nada. The revolution is expansion of self. Evolution. I am an evolutionary.

This is the only way to not succumb to the perceived evils of society. Those Capitalist, Imperialist, Communist, Socialist, Nationalist, Fundamentalist, (did I leave anyone out?), and all other political beasts, cannot destroy a Spirit attuned with its higher self. The societal collective fear is FOOD for the very monster that devours hope and extinguishes the light of the human soul. **Ha! It's not gonna get ME!** It's tried countless times in every type of abstract situation life could muster, but I emerge victorious EVERY TIME...stronger, lighter and happier!!!!

7 Febrero

My cabin is not insulated from the sound of weather. Currently, torrential rains deluge the forest around me, pounding the roof. The sound of the creek rushing with the rising water runs through me, emptying me of all *mind*. My placement in this lights the path that leads outside the *self*. It merges the '*me*' into the ocean from which we all came and still inhabit, despite our forgetfulness and endless distractions.

The scent of lemongrass emanating from the pot atop my woodstove is invigorating as the blazing fires release the fragrance from its oil in the steaming water. Peace and warmth embrace this cottage that is my home, and I within it.

"Ave" is coming out. Ave is *me*. I resonate with that sound. Franz Schubert's "Ave Maria" has been my favorite musical piece (technically, a 'lieder') since childhood. Beyond the shadow of a doubt, this sound resonated as my name, and introduced itself to me in Argentina.

The presence of Che has become peaceful with me. I feel his rage dissolve as I find my equilibrium with acceptance that this is something I'm aligned to be working *with*. Not a tangent into the wilds of an overactive, imbalanced imagination. There is a reason for our union and my calm center will reveal it fully when I step off the rollercoaster of fear and insecurity that is running it's course of being healed. When a defensive thought comes up, I perceive a frustration outside myself, creating that sense of pressure in my face again, but these times are no longer frightening or menacing. I sense just a little sadness within the intensity of the frustration, like someone who is trying to teach something very important and the student just doesn't get it and refuses to look deeper. It's not 'human sadness', that being the closest word I can use to describe this indescribable telepathic transmission. I can physically feel the pressure of his energetic field being in close proximity with mine. He feels my openness to this and I feel his love and appreciation for my continued efforts.

★ THE MISSION AWAKENS ★

<u>11 Febrero</u>
<u>11:11 P.M.</u>

Feelings of anger and depression surfaced after a satisfying dinner and massage, running an extremely uncomfortable course through me. That my relaxing massage unleashed such intense emotions was disappointing. I sense a release in this emotional indicator of disappointment as simply being old stuff bubbling to the surface to vacate my energetic premises. Ahhh, expansion!

Desires for relaxing and melting into mindlessness after receiving this healing touch was overridden with the momentum of my personal evolution blasting forth, expanding!

The priorities I've set in working to complete The Pigeon Chronicles and allowing contentedness with my job is not in accordance with my true purpose. It feels contrary to some force within me creating unbearable restlessness. I feel like it's right in front of my *face* and I'm *MISSING* it. Maybe I'm not missing it at all because I see and feel myself not resonating with what I thought I was to take action on. This restlessness is an indicator that energy is moving and I AM getting it. I'm honoring that taking this planned action is not resonating with me despite what I 'thought' and am 'standing by' to receive direction from the source which is aligned with who I really am.

If this whole ghostly presence *IS* real, then why the *hell* don't I get some obvious sign like people get in the movies? Something *cool* instead of this tormenting invisible stuff!

In the moments thinking this, I 'receive':

"This is not about receiving information you call signs through your five senses to satisfy the illusion of further human yearning."

Man oh man, he's so to the point!

<u>12 Febrero</u>
<u>5:45 A.M.</u>

A tsunami of fear washes over me in my moment of awakening. Anything this intense jolting me out of sleep deserves detached observation rather than resistance and wishing for comfort as I was wrenched out of a terrifying nightmare.

Dreams of ambushing two people I had conflict with years ago. *Ambush.* What the *hell* is up with *that* line of thinking? The details were clear, chilling and *very* out of character for me. It was so disturbing I will not write the details in this journal even for *eventual* recall.

I crave the freedom from wondering what *more* I SHOULD do. There would *be* no choices, I'd simply know it and be clear with my direction. Looks like the fear based ego monster has blindsided me from out of the shadows once again. It only SEEMS there's no slaying this thing, and it is my fears that see this as a monster.

My heart says there's nothing to slay, nothing to resist. It is time to ALLOW myself to listen and accept what my higher self is telling me. It is my resistance that is the dragon. To TRUST in what my higher self is conveying will be to know peace and self-confidence. To accept that my essential nature beats to a rhythm often misunderstood and judged by others and to own that uniqueness without caring what anyone thinks of me, will liberate me and illuminate my path and purpose.

Despite moments of lofty bliss and oneness with the illusive Creator, I have peace of mind only in fleeting moments. "Itchy pants", my parents called me, wishing I could be content with settling down. To me settling down is death for an adventurous spirit curious about life, the world, and energies we don't see.

In my former relationship, I did have a *glimpse* of feeling *'this was it'*. After his voluntary proclamation appointing himself father of my adult daughters "for the rest of their lives" and grandpa to Emma, *'our granddaughter'*, I actually trusted him and didn't wonder what else I *should* be doing other than tending to his "big, important life". I felt settled with being his partner, assistant, gardener, resident hostess and other roles too numerous to recall. After settling into the illusion of being secure with this lifestyle, his mental abuse became corrosive to my spirit.
Lying in bed beside this mistaken love of my life, I received a clear (and what I deemed disturbing at the time) transmission in the wee hours as he lay contently sleeping:

"This man needs to have a son. You are not the mother, it is not your path nor would you want this path. There are other plans for which you have been groomed and resonate with for this expansion. You are on the frequency of an entirely different calling than being this man's perceived partner. You are ripe for the next phase, and we stand by with joyful anticipation when you outwardly choose to make the move. Only the blood-son can continue him on the path you were sent to open. You opened it. Your time with him has expired."

So much for going back to sleep! For some time, I pretended I hadn't heard this information and found myself hanging on to the disintegrating relationship. The tighter I clasped trying to please him, the crueler his words became. On the day my sister's pregnant daughter died, he insisted I move out of our home with neither a discussion nor a word of compassion for this unexpected, horrific loss in my family. My state of shock was equal to the grief of both losses.

Here I am, re-narrating to myself the past that wreaked some of the worst emotional havoc I have EVER known in the arena of alleged love! Must be another round of cleansing out the old layers of sludge energy wedged into the depths of my cellular memory.

A thought constantly hovering in my headspace that I'm not DOING what I was BORN to do is creating a restlessness that is trying to 'tell me something'. It's *more* than the pigeon book, there's something I'm *missing.* I LOVE the idea and my work on the pigeons, and will still produce it in tandem with whatever else turns out to be calling me. **It better speak up soon, I'm all ears and running out of patience!**

As irony dictates, the transmission I received was fully accurate as I just received word last night that this former partner's new wife is pregnant with their son.

My 'receiving apparatus' is in full working order and I need to currently focus that attention on ME, to uncover the mystery of my true directional priority. One thing I know for sure, my invisible friend is here for a reason and the roller coaster of doubt and ecstasy is perhaps the only ride I'm to be on right now as I'm expanding at light speed.

★ ANCESTORS AND LABYRINTHS ★

13 Febrero

Organizing my bookshelf, I rediscovered the beautiful collection of old letters, photos and a segment of our family tree. This family information included many names from the ancestral line mi Tio Luis sent me from his native Puebla, Mexico many years ago. I cherish this piece of family history, and decided to investigate further. **(Tio = uncle in Spanish)**

I went online and Googled the name of my father's older brother. Scrolling back through the decades and centuries, my inner explorer was having a jolly time. It took me outside myself and into that other world ruled by Creation, Inspiration and Imagination.

The distraction from my current nerve-racking reality was refreshing as I time traveled through a lineage containing *all* the names mi tio included in his letters. *Coincidence???*

I explored another Spanish lineage, traveling the dusty trail of its many lives lived to see how common these names might have been.
Few appeared most did not. My family name,
de Velasco, was woven throughout the tapestry of this family tree.
I was mesmerized as this line went back to the 1500's.
When my eyes scanned some names, dates and
relationships, a chill went through me, subtle, but detectable.

There in the late 1590's within the same line segment of lives intertwined in relationship, appeared Guevara and de Velasco.

The chill that ran through me upon reading that was *not* subtle. Could this be that sign I was demanding just two days before? I'm neither superstitious nor in a blind hurry to be shown a sign in something that's not a sign at all if it's a pure, unadulterated black and white coincidence, but this stood the hairs on the back of my neck straight up. I never have believed in coincidences.

14 Febrero
The Day of Lovers

Few are the ones for whom this day will bring no twinge of emotion, be it nostalgic, disappointment or bliss. This day no longer holds a strong charge for me as in years gone by.

I have been craving the sound of beautiful Spanish dialog. *Yearning* to hear it, *yearning* to speak it and immerse myself within it.

Off to be merry on this "evening for lovers", meeting my friend Renoir. Yes, yes, descendant of the master artist, and with the personnalite' d'un artiste Francais. He is a gas to hang out with, always fun, and our intellectual attraction makes us good teatime companions.

We laugh at the silliness of Valentine's Day chocolates and flowers as we go off to enjoy the latest big screen movie, *"Pan Labyrinth"*. Hearing it contained much fantasy and was well produced, I knew nothing of the storyline.

Upon driving to meet Renoir at the cinema, I had unprovoked feelings of intense, pure, unadulterated love emanate out of my core, enveloping me and projecting outward to everyone that crossed my mind.

So encompassing was this 'sensation', I experienced an altered state of consciousness. I was able to safely drive, though this took me quite by surprise. I got into the wave and rode on my surfboard of bliss from behind the steering wheel of my truck.

I felt flooded with Divine electricity throughout my entire body/mind during this experience, and received this:

"Now just **hold** this energy and everything will ease into place. Give us something to work with. Allow the Guidance to take over and the energy you need to go through the necessary motions will be abundant, as will everything else."

"Geez, I'm just driving to a movie for Christ sakes!"

Was it just my state of mind causing me to project onto this movie what my own vibration was resonating? The theme of the movie was the revolutionary struggle. The main character depicting the fearless hero of the oppressed was cast to be reminiscent of Che, possessing the Che sense of 'command' we can read was part of his greatness. *Coincidence?*

I had no idea this movie was spoken in beautiful Castilian Spanish, subtitled for Gringos. The sound was music to my ears! I did not read many subtitles as I sat there mesmerized by the beauty of the sound of this language and the images before my eyes.

When the movie ended, I felt like I received a Valentine's Day gift sweeter than any chocolate, more fragrant than any bouquet from my invisible friend and guides. To say I was pleasantly surprised would win the grossest understatement of the year award, and finding my way out of the theater to my truck I was in yet *another* altered state! This was without question an obvious validation for my persistence on the track in search of clarity. *I couldn't miss it if I were blindfolded.*

★ MY UNEXPECTED LIFE ★

<u>16 Febrero</u>

Am I just trying to convince myself I don't *need* or *want* a man to love me? Are the old war wounds of love so deep that I'm *using* Spirit as a crutch to replace that good old-fashioned *yearning* I could be in denial of having? Ah, there's the old programming again, questioning my potential growing beyond yearning and into a clearer resonance with my own Source being! The human egoic aspect really won't let go, where's my 'override' key?

I need to *complete* the writing and illustrations of The Pigeon Chronicles, creating the satisfaction from meeting a goal that seems out of reach. Distractions of all kinds threaten incompletion, and I battle them with the artillery of my focus.

This morning I am longing for the touch of a loving, sensual partner, the one of my dreams. **Why can't my *ghost* have a body?**

Having chosen unavailable partners on one level or another my entire life, my ghost takes the cake as the epitome of unavailable. Another distraction? I prefer *direction* with focus, tenacity and accomplishment! **No more distractions--not even invisible ones!**

★ ★ ★

<u>10:30 P.M.</u>

With anger purging through me for no apparent reason, I engage with intense prayer to retrieve my center. Recognizing this emotion as obsolete programs running out of habit, I put this energy to work organizing and completing mundane tasks.

With total inner restlessness and self-flagellation of ***do more, do more***, the fear dragon pounced from the shadows and I slayed it yet again! The slaying of these dragons is a victory mistaken, as they merely retreat to my shadows long enough to trick me into thinking I've killed them, then they pounce again when I'm unaware of their continued power over me. It is imperative I keep my machete of awareness sharpened.

Worked on some illustrations for The Pigeon Chronicles, drawing calms the mind.

Tonight Che's presence is *delightfully* intense. The essence of it feels 'soft' and *affectionate*. There are no words to accurately describe this feeling surrounding me from *outside* myself. As my mind opens and acceptance grows knowing there is a clear purpose to this, there is a shift in his energetic presence. Ahhhhh, EASE!

Two close friends who know me well but not each other were finally told of my 'invisible friend'. Before disclosure of my situation and upon their separate visits, each 'felt' something and said to me *"who's here with you? It feels like someone is in your cabin."*
One thing for sure—I have NOT been alone in my cabin sanctuary since I returned from Argentina.

His presence bestows *tenderness*, and ecstasy is ***given*** to me. In these euphoric moments, I'm rendered immovable, my sensory receptors being filled to perceived capacity. Awareness of this *being a gift* of *pure love* fills my consciousness, bypassing all intellectual processes and perceptions. This rapture usually lasts an interval of seconds, but the subtle bliss lingers long after. Literary attempts describing these events are positively inadequate, but the writer in me is compelled to grasp for the words chronicling these experiences despite the limited verbiage available.

How many people out there is something even *similar* to this *authentically* happening? I mean *REALLY!!!* And if it *is*, do they think they are going crazy, trying to ignore it, getting medication or writing books, going on tour and being keynote speakers for groups interested in the paranormal? I tire of questioning the validity of this experience and my sanity. I am at peace only in the moments I don't resist, and allow and acknowledge this reality as my true experience. This in and of itself tells me I'm barking up the right tree.

19 Febrero
Sunset

Looking forward to my appointment today with a professional healing facilitator. My intention for this session is to work on the chronic pain in my right shoulder and explore what's going on with my invisible friend. It's time for some open-minded healing professional to help me sort this out and retrieve my logical mind if in fact it needs retrieving.

Session:

Shoulder: deals with strength & flexibility.
She 'strengthened my aura to keep out any unwanted energies' and to let in those only in the best interest of my highest good.

My eyes are to remain closed during the session. I of course take an occasional peak, seeing nothing unusual.

She said that the constant and close presence of this energy that I sense to be Che is causing an irritation in my auric field. When she spoke these words *a strong presence came into the room* we both felt. She then spoke with a sharp tone as she addressed it, "either go into the light or leave and go elsewhere." I immediately felt the presence to be my ghost. She continued her work on me. I guess he chose to not go into the light as I felt him leave.

The session complete, shoulder pain was almost GONE! Her last words to me upon leaving were: "Think about which route to drive home—whichever one came into your mind first is the one (there are several ways to go). Drive directly home with no detours. **The message was to take it safe."**

When I walked out to my vehicle through her garden that emanated safety and tranquility, I found Mr. Invisible waiting for me in my truck, his energetic countenance was **'all smiles'**. I was happy with him being there, and wondered if this occurrence provoked the practitioner's intuition, hence her last words of taking it safe.

Coming away with my mind open, empty, and in the presence of 'the presence', the thought filled me that my connection with this spirit is not exclusively his Che Guevara incarnation, but from a shared lineage on the revolutionary flow of consciousness and an aspect I am part of and resonate with. It is not a revolution utilizing firearms and warfare. **As he transmitted this information to me, there was clearly an indescribable love woven within our interaction, and it is positively delicious when I don't resist it.**

★ MY NAME AND PURPOSE ★

23 Febrero

This is the 2nd anniversary of the death of my niece, the death of my love relationship and the family we created by our coming together. These anniversaries evoke intense feelings of grief and loss, a human process of healing I'm OK with. I will allow the emotional tide to rise and recede without resistance or wallowing.

24 Febrero

Pouring rain, very cold. I love this weather from inside my warm cabin.

So persistent is my desire for an honest evaluation of what is actually happening here with this ghost, who has revealed to me to *actually be* the essence of the former Che Guevara, I called my long time friend for a session who's worked on my family and me for many years. I simply *must get some guidance* from a long established specialist in energetic healing. He's a very different sort of practitioner than the one who worked on my shoulder. He works with guides and achieves results with even his most skeptical new patients. He has a popular, long established practice including many techniques for working with the innate wisdom and inner healer inherent in us all. He can also give the best chiropractic adjustment money can buy.

Session w/ Dr. JS
A M A Z I N G

Che to Dr. JS: "I didn't have to be a revolutionary
in the ways I was. I carry regret
for the things I have done."

"Martyrdom is overrated."

Notes from session:
He is with me because of "an ancient connection, our harmonic resonance, and
because I am not of a
limited, narrow mind."

That said, Dr. JS put hands up to simulate the blinders on a horse saying, "It is because
you are not like this."

"Che was blocked behind a 'wall', and thru this session done 'for him thru me', he is free to go and work on the levels he's needed to with others, and is appreciative of my bringing him to the table for healing."

"This session unlocked him. He's free." This is what JS told me he 'received'.
Back home in my cabin, I hear a tree crash to the ground somewhere close in the woods as I write these words.

Spiritual Revolutionary. I hear my ghost remind me I am this. I know I have always been this.

I feel so clear and 'smooth', it's like I'm *invisible*. There's no other way to describe the sensations I am experiencing.

The rain is positively torrential!!! The name dances in my mind and across the pages of my journal:

AVE GUEVARA de VELASCO

AVE GUEVARA de VELASCO---when this name segment fills my mind, I can "feel" a resounding "YES!" from the invisibles. This is the name *he* invited me to assume with my acceptance of our union. These are received thoughts, not coming from my own mind, but coming *through* it.

After any session with Dr. JS, there is always a segment of time I *go within*, retreat to my sanctuary and 'digest' what has occurred. I'm feeling particularly close with my spirit companion after this session, that closeness being our energies *merging* rather than the closeness of two humans in love. Similar yet different.

Without the usual bombardment of questioning I present over the validity of this situation, I feel relaxed and just allow it all to *BE*. It is in this quiet, empty space that I usually 'receive information'.
(I also receive information out in nature when my mind is 'empty' taking walks)

During this particular quiet time I 'received' the new name I am to assume matching the molecular shift my cellular matrix has undergone since the Argentine journey. I am 'told' this name is given to me by my invisible companion and agreed upon by my own guides. I receive the following transmission from my guides:

"He invites you to take the name of his former incarnation, expanding the resonance that has been recognized between your morphic fields. There is work with which assuming this name will assist. Resonant sounds, what humans call 'names' carry a power misunderstood by the human mind. You understand this power and the power of sound, hence you have accepted changes in your resonant sounds before this present invitation. This will be a work of healing for him from his actions in the perceived past involving others on a global scale that he has carried forth into non physical and desires to move beyond and expand from. This work is necessary for the evolution of his soul and the souls of others who are stuck in their grief and hatred. This healing contributes to the expansion of humanity. He senses he has work to do to assist in the healing of those affected both living and not living on earth presently, and you are the human vehicle that resonates with and is equipped to facilitate this work. Assuming his name promotes a necessary psychic, personal and material bond which contributes to this expansion. As the human aspect of this union, you have the need for external manifestations of the spiritual bond. This need is honored by us, as is your openness, willingness and human nature. You are his spiritual partner for the evolution of both your souls, and your evolution and expansion will extend out to the lives of many."

"That name is Ave Guevara de Velasco."

The sound of this name resonates with me completely and unquestionably. There is no gray area of questioning. This feels in complete harmony with my energetic field, logical mind and heart. I feel solid with this beyond question, and it feels like '***home***'. I can relax now with the knowledge that was both exciting and unsettling, knowing this was coming. Changing names for any reason is a significant process, as it changes the vibration of the named.

✶ ACCEPTANCE = EXPANSION ✶

25 Febrero
Sunday Morning

This is my favorite day of the week, weather and time of day. Awaiting tea, fire warming, raining and blustery outside. I am in total peace after last night's first and *very long* session with JS regarding this situation. I am uncomfortably consumed with it, and research for concrete answers is imperative to my personal wellbeing. Quite frankly, this invasion is unwelcome and the word distraction doesn't begin to describe this multi-dimensional roller coaster ride, but it doesn't go away and I don't know if I will ever have my life as it was before this integration.

Feeling the need to be quiet. No phone, no discussions, no dissertations on the 'whys' of it all. Life change and death anniversaries are intense and I need to take the non-productive edge off. My niece and her unborn baby died the same day the family unit dissolved that my daughter's and I felt safe with - it's been two years since this upheaval and transition.

Experiencing major frustration and moments of craziness over the Che presence AGAIN. Another level of fear is up for clearing. Many fears at night, as in the darkness people seem to be at their weakest ebb. It's a generic feeling of fear for no situation or detail in particular. I have never had anything like this occur in my life, and have never desired paranormal experiences. I was developing a new career as travel writer and photographer when this detour blindsided me. Everything is for a reason, even if I don't fully understand the Divine reasoning. The dips and peaks of *this ride* stabilize as I accept myself to be the receiver of this unseen force and relax behind my incessant questioning of this experience's validity. I cannot seem to *maintain* acceptance. **It's all just too bizarre even for me!**

It feels like the molecular levels of my cellular composition have all been cleaned, oiled and adjusted. My clarity renders me so clear as to have sustained this feeling of 'invisibility' since the session with JS. Invisible is a word that only remotely describes a feeling impossible to classify. I can't believe I'm even writing descriptions such as these regarding my own self!

His spirit is free. His presence around me is calmer, and we are bonded through his appreciation of my continued work with him, not discounting it to insanity or imagination, but believing this is happening, as well as my acceptance of our remote link no matter how 'crazy' this may sound to anyone outside my inner circle. **This is not a random experience, there IS a purpose.**

He and I have work to do, and as long as I remain without even a pet he will be with me. I am told this in no uncertain terms:

"No boy friend, not even a pet".

I have full range of motion in the shoulder that has been causing me chronic discomfort. I am nurturing myself with yoga postures, homemade soup and cornbread today. Confidence replaces fear. My 'ally' is working on the other side. Spirit is working through me and prayers for ultra-focused motivation continue. I am settling in with acceptance of the reality of this most unconventional situation.

I don't want Che to *ever* leave when the love and ecstasy flows and my love capacity expands with this presence.

27 FEBRERO
11:22 A.M.

Receiving direction on steps to take regarding the work to be done on my property include creating a retreat where clients can choose from a 'menu' of healing modality combinations.

Hold the integrative space for the client and their own 'inner healer'. Offer choice of healing packages. 1-3 day retreats, organic meals served. Reservations seasonal. Book early.

Soil and plant therapy- -hands in earth and the gardens to be included 'on the menu'.
Put teepee or some simple structure either on or near the island surrounded by the running waters of the creek.

Ave Guevara de Velasco – –
Musician/Artist/Writer/Photographer/Host for the energetic healing of the spirit that inhabited Ernesto 'Che' Guevara. His healing will extend out to the souls of those living and not living who were affected by the actions of his infamous past incarnation...I review the channeling from a few days ago. Sounds good, sounds crazy also, everyone will think I am delusional when this comes out. Maybe I'll just get a new puppy and be done with it!

RECEIVED THIS "TRANSMISSION":

"Not 'Che' as humans perceive. **This is a very important point to stay and center on.** The tendency will be to get lost in aspects of the Che Guevara incarnation. This will be a *huge* distraction. Beware of your human yearnings getting in the way of this work. When you question your sanity you will know you have slipped off course."

* *   End of transmission   * *

My own mind speaks up at this point, and this is MY mind, MY thoughts, and MY question. It sparks a response from the other realm.

Me to self: "Oh yeah, so you *really* think you want this continued and deepening connection???"

"This is what comes with it.

It's **Your** choice, Ave. It's the continued work upon which you both resonate, hence joining to participate with. Attention will be both favorable and seemingly unfavorable....
Earthly woman and the Source spirit who's prior earthly incarnation was that of Che Guevara."

I was minding my own business in Argentina intending to 'clear my plate' of past heartache and prepare for my new, improved life and career, then **POW**. This.

OK, *I WANT MY LIFE BACK;* not the one with the heartache, but the one I anticipated having *after* my trip, that life I had intentionally focused on. I have no recollection of even remotely implying my desire for a paranormal experience, and I did not 'ask the universe' for a partner of any kind, in body or not. My intent to develop a travel-writing career must have been interpreted by the Creative Force to mean writing about travels **within** of a very different nature than earthly adventures to faraway places with pretty photographs. I'm definitely writing about travel, but they are journeys extending to my cellular depths and adventures involving **another dimension**!

"Fun ride, great imagination, now go and get a poodle or a goldfish," I tell myself. (It turns out to not come with this option.) Upon these thoughts, I hear:

"This IS the direction you've been seeking. Think back to your 20's.

You've always *been* part of a revolution. To seek liberation within the *self is truly revolutionary. You are a revolutionary.*

Using guns was only one fraction of experience within the nature of soul's eternal life. Mistaking the revolutionary fighter within us all to be AGAINST change **within oneself**, it was a battle projected onto others by use of warfare.

It now has to be recognized for what it is. The governments can change only if the masses change them*selves* and feel the birthright of their *own* empowerment. To do the work to acquire perfect health within the body/mind for maximum clarity is essential for empowerment.

Liberate the self from limiting thought patterns. The more people doing this will eventually spread it, fingering out through the web of humanity and touching all lives ------------
e v e n t u a l l y

     It will touch everyone

     It is not about politics, religion, acquiring power or a belief system

     It's not about genetic predisposition, or being dealt an oppressed hand in the card game of life

     Persevere   NO MATTER WHAT
              ANYBODY ELSE THINKS

Set the example of how it's done by channeling the inherent source or creative power throughout your entire cellular being. From continued perseverance in KNOWING and expressing that knowledge by *allowing* your Divine Nature, you will assist with the momentum that will bring about this change. The physical manifestation of this will touch many lives currently asking to be shaken awake. Holding this space will assist in the awakening.

The ammunition for this perceived fight in this shift is proper nutrition. This is so basic it is overlooked. People in your current homeland are fed too much toxic food and fearful information and remain malnourished both physically and spiritually. The surface of the planet is as poisoned as the inhabitants. Operating from this place robs the soul of awareness of its beauty and empowerment. People want the solution to be something more complicated.

Changing destructive habits and focusing on that which awakens positive thought-forms is something most people are not willing to do despite knowing that it will change the quality of their life and that of their children. It takes more work and perseverance than the masses are willing to put forth, they are basically lazy. This laziness is rooted in their toxic bodies and minds. Your incarnation, Ave, has the potential to assist in this shift, and the invisibles are guiding you.

It will take courage to step into Ave Guevara."

★ THAT SAID . . . ★

1 March

Frozen snow on ground crunches beneath my feet. Healing retreat idea gaining momentum. **Ave Guevara:** I *love* her, she's *ME*, *I love me* ! A new sound and identity to step in to, reflecting the 'me' that is now outside any and **all** familiar boxes. Shifting vibrations and frequency.

4 March
Sunday

DREAM: Some people and I were playing in elevators beneath the World Trade Towers. I got too close to the edge and slipped, hanging onto an edge looking down far below into crevices and a certain dismal, painful death. Couldn't scream or utter any sound at all, as ANY bodily vibration, even vocal chord use and I'd fall. A lady walked beneath and I couldn't get her attention. My death was imminent.

Woke up feeling relieved and *so* glad to be in my bed.

Annmarie bought me dinner last night at the local authentic Chilean restaurant. Che clearly ordered dinner, and I felt myself allowing him to **use my body** for the total experience. I cannot utilize language to convey the sensations when he occupies the same space as me. My body is the vehicle utilized to house two beings from two dimensions into one vibrational essence.

Skewered tri tip is not something on any menu that appeals to my personal taste nor would I ever order it. Having a distinct South American flavor, I felt his genuine enjoyment at ordering and devouring the meal. Together we felt comfortable, had F U N and there was a sense of peace with the integration. **This was a *first*.**

He's my 'official' companion now, and my closest lady friends ask about him as if he's my new love interest. In this newly awakened reality, he actually IS my new love interest. I kind of like that. We'll see what comes of this. I have been assigned a stout mission, or more accurately, I've been awakened to my full potential, and I've agreed to be fully awake. **Recollection of this requires the vigilant work of a full-time Warrior.**

His presence was very strong with me the night before when Brandy, Emma and I went out for Mexican food. My ghost seems to enjoy big dinners served in restaurants.

Sunday afternoon

Channeled dialog between ghost & me:

"Shake it. Move the body. Dance.
Infuse Ave with HER life. Feel **US**."

"I can't SEE you!"

"With earthly eyes, I am not physically visible. You are not physically visible to me, I don't have earthly eyes or earthly vision, but I feel you fully"
Trust what you know- - Stop fearing insanity.

This phase of your purpose only FEELS LONELY from the human aspect of your being."

"But I AM human!"

"Don't limit your perception to being only a human, human-ness is only a current and partial manifestation of your entire being, you do not yet fully realize the entirety of what you really are."

I get a sense of being soothed and stroked lovingly.
There is a calm 'tone' as a gentle, loving parent (spirit) to the agitated baby (me).

"Your mate from the soul group doesn't have a body now. This condition is by choice. It *found* **YOU**. Your point-of-being emanated a certain light, color, brightness, frequency, whatever you call it, but your conditions were aligned to be a beacon for him to find you through the matrix of creation."

This communication came to me during my *conversation* with my ghost, from my life-guides.

Now we have our continued work in a very different format than the human to human, boy meets girl, have children and a dog in the yard. This is definitely not the card I have been dealt this lifetime.

"We are not that now, darling.
I've been here all along. Now you know it and no, you are not insane. I do not come from your insanity or imagination.

And yes, your part in the vision of the planetary shift involves utilizing the resources given you for this purpose--music-art-writing-healing. This is your reality now. It's always been there but now you are awakened to it."

It's not MY dream. I'm involved IN the vision. We are spokes of the same wheel. (I've always felt myself to be a spoke rather than the whole wheel)

"Stop worrying and allow yourself to accept your power/attune-ness.

Stop wondering. NO, YOU'RE NOT INSANE. This fear is holding you up. It's taking your energy, and that's why your perceived ability to DO THIS is compromised. It's being consumed to deal with the presence and persistence of this continued fear. Yes, it's seems to you to be dying hard. But it doesn't *DIE*, it *transforms* when it merges with the DIVINE, when you consciously give up your diseased affiliation with EGO. We can all play together here. Humans call it work and make it out to be difficult and struggle."

*   *   *

This channeled conversation ends, and the room here in my sanctuary is absolutely PACKED with Angelic beings. They are *all looking at me*. They are embracing and infusing me with this information. I cannot deny the reality of this experience for any reason.

Right now, on this blank page in my journal, I seem to be writing very fast. It's just me holding the pen here, placing myself completely out of the way of what's writing THROUGH my hand. Is that called scribing? Time to 'birth' Ave Guevara.

"Stop thinking you're crazy, dear. Go take a walk."

11 Marzo
Sunday morning

Feeling Divine presence fully. Shoulder pain gone. Che and I growing strong with the Divine purpose we are awakened to that can only be accomplished from my being in a body and his not. I'm feeling the momentum.

God realization seems to happen one molecular crumb at a time. We're all just molecules anyway. I've felt this way since 4th grade science class first learning molecules existed. Light one or dark one? God or Ego empowered? We seem to need assigned tasks, why not have it be a task on the Divine list? Lots of healing for that incarnation called Che Guevara, not just for him, but also for the one's who's lives his actions altered. This is an interesting and fascinating piece and one I never saw coming. Through allowing this healing I will also be healed, and *I certainly need some healing right now!*

Saturated with love, this understanding soothes the fear monster shadow of insanity. 'Communications received' have clearly confirmed it's a situation of right time, place, mind resonance and alignment.

★ CHE'S NEW NAME ★

15 Marzo

Walked with a friend to the waterfalls. We sensed Che's amusement at her inability to cross the creek. She 'hears' Che infuse words directly to her:

"She and I did this, we do this." (with this communication came the *knowledge* he was referring to me)

While sitting at the falls my friend spontaneously says, "He's going to manifest". Says I, "But I'm attached to how we are now. It's perfect, actually, I don't *want* him to manifest into a body." (bodily manifestation was my assumption)

My friend and I sat on the beach a long time; the energy was electric amidst the serenity of the falls. Che's presence was evident and strong. Empty mind, I was in ecstasy just *being*, feeling his energy flow through my body, vibrate every cell and drift out again.

"I'm not ready for the manifestation, my own career success needs to be launched first. I can't believe it can really be as good as it is with him right now *not* being in a body. I love my ghost the way he is." No mortal has ever come 'through' me and amalgamate with my energy in the way that he does. The best companionship or sex never came close to *this* oneness.

It came through at the waterfall and I spontaneously announced, "He wants to be called something other than Che. He doesn't want me too connected with that incarnation, it's not *him* anymore."
(I've already read enough about Che Guevara to have some connection established)

Upon returning from the falls, I was moved to find the old hiking boots I replaced years ago with a lightweight version, never having the heart to give away my clunkers. I felt him 'light up' at finding them, and was moved to polish and wear them. They cleaned up rather nicely, and their weight would add to my walking workout. I also found my big old rusty knife I hadn't used in years, and was moved to clean that up as well. I 'heard' dialog about the "value of good boots" from my invisible companion.
I had a decent studio session w/my friend Renoir. I'd been struggling on previous sessions to get this vocal track down, and tonight had it acceptable within 45 minutes. Although the project was eventually scrapped, I still feel music inside me that needs to be expressed.

We went to dinner after the session, and I felt myself filled with the familiar energy and he was **so** enjoying the meal, that my dinner partner noticed my eyes rolling with a look come over my face not unlike that of a woman having an orgasm. **He said he'll "never forget that look I had over just eating spaghetti!"** I will never forget that *feeling*. With no question I was partially out-of-body while sharing my body with the energy of my ghost. We were BOTH in there.

16 March
1 A.M.

Went to bed asking for concrete, easily understood answers to my situation with the presence that never seems to leave me, and am awakened by a dream. Still dreamy sleepy, I reach for pen & journal, driven to write the remnants before they evaporate.

DREAM: Guerilla activity in the woods. No bloodshed. Details are gone, but the FEELING from the images stays strong with me. The feeling was oneness with the powerful essence of Commandante Guevara.

I spontaneously remembered he *told* my friend at the falls that–

"He was going give me strength and courage".

* * *

Ready for my 3-hill run routine. Nourished my body with apples, pears, toast and mate'-drinking it from the traditional gourd. As I was deciding to have màte instead of my beloved Earl Grey, the thought occurred it may please my invisible friend in some way, considering he had such an addiction to it in the past incarnation I'm not supposed to focus on.

He says emphatically (and I heard it with a Spanish accent!): "I don't give a **SHEET** anymore about mate`, I do this for you because you need that connective validating ritual." I felt his energy sporting a big, adoring smile. This was actually *fun!*
The interaction felt essentially affectionate.

Bits of received information from the day at the falls with my friend filter back to me, and I remember the dialog verbatim:

"The connection flows directly with this land and water, your physical placement out here is the vibration conducive to this interaction, hence your call to live out in nature".

The presence and connection I so vigorously feel is always confirmed while outside in any capacity, be it cutting wood, planting trees, taking walks or exploring down at the water.

Becoming Ave, stepping INTO her has taken huge, consistent doses of courage to actually be doing. I'll be filing name change papers today. Filling out the papers before sleep last night was intentional action on a decision that's required much attention and focus.

Opened my Course in Miracles to a random page (that's how I read most books). The page was the Holy Relationship Introduction. I couldn't believe the words my eyes absorbed describing the essence of this union I am experiencing with this invisible, yet very real companion. (♥*Notes)*

The level of relating and oneness between us seems beyond that of an intimate relationship between two mortals due to the dynamic interference of the baggage, history and individual issues inherent between humans. It's becoming stronger, clearer and gaining momentum. Always 'for the highest good'- - I repeat that with conviction frequently to *keep* clear! The ego is THAT tricky. **It tricks me every time I question this situation or my mental stability.**

For humans, the yearnings, thoughts and drive for getting what we think we need completely smokescreens truth. The pursuit of satisfying these conditions thickens the smokescreen immensely.

At this phase of life, I seek truth more than fulfillment of human yearnings. (I've spent excessive time and energy in my youth thinking fulfillment of noble human yearnings and relationships as part of the point in being here!) That's not to say human yearnings don't sneak in and distract me now, I'm certainly far from overcoming *that* completely! All relations are food for our soul's expansion.

In this unlikely and unexpected union, what I have become and am becoming through it leaves the best romantic human relationship I've ever experienced *ABSOLUTELY IN THE DUST!*

The thought of serving another human male ego completely BORES me and does not promote my service to the highest good for myself or anyone else.

I take Sunday afternoon tea upon my deck steeped in deep gratitude. My life's entire process thus far is proof of Divine essence and the power of focused clarity. I'm relaxing a little on this insanity factor and 'trying on' how it feels to accept that this *really is* happening *with me* and not *to me.* Serenity settles in my bones.

My world has completely changed since Argentina!

The sound "Vea" (pro: vay'-ah) fills my consciousness. With an unexplained knowledge revealed to me, this is what my ghost is to be referred to rather than Che. The resonant sound of his spirit (aka-'name') is VEA, not Ernesto or Che. So we both expanded into a new resonant sound!

ACIM♥ Notes: "A holy relationship starts from a different premise. Each one has looked within and seen no lack. Accepting his completion, he would extend it by joining with another, whole as himself. He sees no difference between these selves, for differences are only of the body. Therefore, he looks on nothing he would take. He denies not his own reality because it is the truth. Just under Heaven does he stand, but close enough not to return to earth. For this relationship has Heaven's Holiness. How far from home can a relationship so like Heaven be?

Reason now can lead you and your brother to the logical conclusion of your union. It must extend, as you extended when you and he joined. It must reach out beyond itself, as you reached out beyond the body, to let you and your brother be joined.

This veil you and your brother lift together opens the way to truth to more than you.

Such is the function of a holy relationship; to receive together and give as you received."

★ THE BIRTH OF AVEA ★

19 Marzo

"So much fear in trusting, my little one!"
    (expressed with affection, not superiority)

"So much continued proof required"
    (a smiling gentleness caressed me)

He's so much gentler since the JS session--more at ease with himself, though still very intense.

I jokingly dared him aloud to find a missing invoice that needed attention if he was *really around.* An exchange of what could only be interpreted from my human receiver as 'laughter' occurred between us after I walked over to one of several random stacks of papers and picked it out of the middle, like a lucky card.

Told today but not by Vea, that I would not feel his presence for some time before he actually manifests. This timing indicated to be only after my success is blossoming, he would be part of that phase as he can guide me with the notoriety that will accompany the mission's success.

I love it this way...

... don't want it to change ~ it's just getting good

as it is finding balance, I am finding myself

I feel him finding himself more as he heals the prior incarnation.   We have safety together
doing this work. It can only be done within
the holy relationship. The two joined are
already there on their own.

Joined by spirit, creator, the unknowable,
God, Yahweh, Source. it has many names.

Holy relationships are not joined by 'finding
each other anywhere on the planet.'
Holy relationships resonate together and that which created each and knows that their place on the path has prepared them for this extension through their union.

To doubt this is to deny all that's been communicated to me throughout my entire
life; so far everything that's ever been

communicated to me this way
has come to pass verbatim.

Why would this time not be so and me
insane instead? I know too much to disbelieve
this knowing.

20 Marzo

Last official day of winter and I spy a sunny spot distant on
the hillside amidst an approaching purple rain front.
Blocked by trees, I am unable to photograph this moment. A
visual gift for my eyes only, and its power and
beauty *is* a *gift* indeed!

Vea. Vea came through as his 'resonant sound'. When I
received this information, I didn't realize that Ave and Vea
complement each other to the extent they do. Repetition of
either name brings on the other.

"Stay off the phone. Too much chatter!   Feel **Me!**"
(I clearly 'hear' this.)

Thinking of Argentina, where our union awakened me and
became conscious. He has invited me to assume this name
and have the courage to stand up, take it and wear it to the
world. Ave Guevara is to step up and out.
Evolutionary & REvolutionary.

A strong urge to crank up my chain saw passes through,
start cutting and thinning trees to enhance the view of that
sun-drenched slope other side of the creek.

Waterfall channeling
First day of spring

Early morning to my island
      exploring without camera. Beneath shrubs with waters
flowing, communications are received,
          powerful and ongoing.

"To doubt the validity of being in holy relationship with Vea
and the union's continuance for highest good, all connected
according to readiness and resonance- - to doubt this or poke
fun at your sanity is to _not be ready._"

The continued work has prepared me.

Incessant doubting undoes the readiness but not the
progress. Acceptance of this new level of existence and
continuing with unfaltering trust is to pass the initiation. I
stand ready.   I accept what most would deem insane. Having
come this far I hope I can pull off the unfaltering part. I fully
accept this holy partner and the creation of this union.
Because the last incarnation of my resonant companion was
an infamous, controversial figure, the challenge is multiplied
to remain unfaltering. It really wouldn't have mattered who
he was, or who I am, there is no doubt in my heart of hearts
the components of this holy union.
I recognized him beyond question in Argentina. He found me
before my awareness of him awakened there.
          I surrender.

The fire heats up as I ease into the coziness of my bed this
early hour. Receiving so much information requires
downtime for energetic recovery. My body is deliciously
exhausted from extinguishing blackberry brambles with my
machete that were threatening to again take over the island.
Victory was mine.

★ CONVERSATIONS WITH VEA ★

22 March

Tea at the table this morning with the *màte* gourd placed honoring Vea.

I empathize with women who still set a place for their dead husband, unable to let go.

This isn't that, though, and I'm reminded of such by the invisibles that are ever present and seem to hear my thoughts. It is more to honor the unseen presence with my own need for human ritual.

26 March

With hot tea on chilled sunny morning, I bask in the contentment within the embrace of Creation.
This situation requires surrender on a daily basis to That which created and sustains the whole show. It's actually quite delicious and juicy when I put down the whole fear thing.

Channeling Spirit's will relieves fear regarding the mundane affairs of life, such as financial security for old age. My girl's wedding date approaches and the planning is a fun diversion from life with my invisible friend. For **me** walking her down (or is it up?) the aisle, balances those 25+ years of single parenting struggles with a joyous grand finale.

... 9 P.M.

The rain pours steady and the fire is blazing, assisting with the integration of the second session with JS for Vea and me. We both received a clearing and balancing, which was needed. In ceremonious gratitude, I changed the bed linens and took an extra long, hot shower before hunkering down. Ah the deliciousness of certain aspects of the human experience!

This love could not possibly be an invention of an idle mind, loneliness or insanity. It's too deep. The healing work done together is beyond the ability of my imagination to have conjured up. I feel his relief at my new schedule having Mondays off work.

"I will have you more to ourselves...we can build momentum...I will help you complete what you need as Ave Guevara."

No mortal man has brought me such profound, unique and complete joy while kicking my ass on a level such as this! It's an immortal ass kicking!

27 March

I need the stamina from my companion's past life or from my 20's.

... 11 P.M.

   either I don't feel his presence as it's integrated another level or we've merged deeper. he seems
         gone, giving me a much needed
            break, or both. his frustration
           (for no better word) at my continued
non-belief and/or recognition of both he and the purpose of his presence and our union, seems somewhat
      diminished as I've grown with this experience.

Whenever I think and/or say it's changed my life or the course of it, I consistently *hear:*

"You just didn't see it...you weren't yet ready for it. You were distracted by human-perceived needs of various illusory situations."

He's been around me for a while now. We resonated and were **joined**; it was not a random meeting of a disembodied soul and open, vulnerable human allowing tramp souls, 'walk-ins' or other paranormal activity.

30 Marzo

My old 'cheer' would kick in after a love gone wrong, *"my soul mate is simply NOT on this planet!"* – to make light and laugh about loves' demise. **Funny how truth is disguised in jokes.**

After so many rounds of disbelief and resistance to this union after all the communications, I sense a stirring from the other side close to frustration. Not the human version of frustration, (that word comes the closest) as there's no words to describe for mortal understanding the feeling and knowing that passes between us.

The human co-dependent tendencies I applied to this holy relationship are invalid upon reflection. Despite clear validation, fears again have arisen of Vea being from imagination. Accumulation of these fears reached its zenith, and in those moments came this:

"You must cease the human habit of boxing this relationship into limited human fear-based perceptions...I have been feeling for the one resonating with this work and that has brought me to you, of this there is no question...we are now **both** aware of this union within each other, joined by the creative force...you are taking my former earthly name and embarking on a journey which will include sacrifice of your perceived invisible status...I am not leaving you now...I will be guiding you through what is to come into your life...you will be needing guidance from this realm, the angelic family, spirit and me...my last incarnation included what you will experience this life...

The work you will be doing with this name is necessary for the experience of my own healing through you...you will experience your own healing through this work and this healing will reach out to the lives of those still living and also those not living on earth who have suffered at the hand of my past incarnations...and others as well...

...your openness of mind to DO this and the work you have done on your own inner progress makes us partners, resonating in spirit, in holy relationship as your book closely describes for you...holy relations don't find each other, they are joined by that which creates all and knows all...spirit *IS* us, therefore knows the depths of mind, soul and intention of each particle...our intention is aligned...i don't *seem* with you at all times, but there is no separation between us...

...as we grow within this union, we extend out to others as this is the natural extension of *spirit* love....we assist others to recognize this in themselves...it's not about the human concept of exclusivity...all concepts: human conditional love, abandonment, betrayal, separation and the *desire* for exclusivity are ego's fear blocking the light source from reaching the soul and liberating it...

...sex, making love, no matter what this act is called, is desire in its densest form to experience the oneness of the union we are, Ave...I am able to merge with your energy field within the body (energy's densest form)...any action humans cling to pales next to this form of union...I realize the difficulty to comprehend, embrace or accept by any human, no matter how open the mind...

...in love?...yes we are with*in* love...we enjoy ultimate shelter within divine union that a human/human union cannot fully know...we know this...stop being in fear of it. Your free will chose this, you forgot you made this choice."

Earlier today, a rainbow prism formed a giant smile arch in the brilliant afternoon sky...it lasted a long time and I took many pictures...upon this viewing came loud & clear:

"Do not judge his killing...maintain no positive judgments either...no judgments of any kind...period...nada.

...allow the liberation from human yearnings, cravings...***drop all of it***."

I've already changed my name and am stepping into this with both feet, complete faith and moments of being scared shitless.

My immunity from the icon status and global following of Che Guevara was another of those conditions aligning me for this union, I am 'told'. Ours is a soul healing, and reading a fraction of all that is written about him has me understand why hosting total ignorance of his existence was a prerequisite for our union to be authentic.

Neutral space, emptiness.

Midnight
Friday/Saturday

Life of non-judgment is difficult practice, as the mind is ingrained with it and diseased from it. Learning of the extensive exploitation of his image and 'what he stood for' creates conflict. Familiarizing with that incarnation holds the dangerous possibility of altering my neutrality and the quality of my participation in this union.

I frequently feel compelled to learn French and Spanish.

31 Marzo

Should death's door open to me *in this moment*, I would leave a perfect life of contentment and happiness.

A Holy Relationship has been awakened, and it's as authentic as my own soul. Source smiles upon me for a life lived with devotion, gratitude and unshakeable faith despite the earthly challenges. It seems I've passed a series of tests. Or maybe it's not about tests and rewards at all, but just the joy felt of expanding beyond previous limitations of mind and perception. Sure feels like a reward though!

Easter Sunday

Thoughts of gratitude on this day awakened memories of the former love relationship stirring angst. Vea points out - - - **"By giving the matter any thought or opinion at all is to give it energy it does not warrant."**

Truly, my thoughts are responded to before I can bat an eye!! Easter finds me resurrected in some ways.

Truly, this union with Vea reflects a completely different union then I've experienced with any mortal, this is a *huge* adjustment for me.

The event with Neal in Aravaipa Canyon's extreme wilderness was a brief visit to this spectrum of interaction with Spirit that is now a daily occurrence.

Though this multi-dimensional relationship is exhilarating and draining simultaneously, I am directed to *not be distracted* by these sensations or what appears to be a roller coaster of knowing it to be true and then filled with the angst of disbelief. The roller coaster effect is simply an old habit, one that no longer serves me, or maybe never served me at all and I didn't see over the hill to the other side!

2 April

Verve. Ecstatic experience. Trusting my instinct when it appears crazy and impossible.
The feeling of being drained is an indication of my own resistance to what is..

Vea's presence is currently strong. Cutting wood is a love/hate thing. Love feeling alive from the exercise it provides and the independence of creating my *own* heat. Hate that it challenges my shoulder and both hands (compromised from a car crash and surgical repairs) grasping the maul, hurts badly when I miss the target. It smashes onto the cutting surface, jolting the hell out of my bones. I love it when I hit and split, and hate it when I miss-which is frequent. I dared my invisible macho soldier that if he indeed *is real*, he will come through me *"right this instant and cut this fucking wood!"*

What followed convinced the inner skeptic beyond any doubts: Without the usual intensity accompanying his visits, I split the wood with a force stronger than I had in my 30's (been using wood heat for a long time)- - I didn't **once** miss the mark, and hopefully without sounding sexist –I cut wood *like a man!* I had a huge pile of perfectly split wood within moments and neither my hands nor shoulder hurt. I thanked my invisible friend with private amazement as I stacked the pile.

. . . 9:40 P.M.

Communication from the other side today had a resonance to it that was Spanish accented male. In all the communications I've ever *received,* there has never been a gender or accent of any kind. They were in fact never even *heard*, but were a *knowing* and an understanding that I *received.* Today this *voice* was heard (but not with my ears):

"Forget the phone, forget your friends...who in the end will be there for you---none of them...

...go home and work for your*self*...writing, artwork, just for you...let it be just **us**...do not get distracted by any person or conversation...be silent and in silence do your work...allow yourself the necessary space to be inspired and create a flow. Momentum is vital. Who in the end will be there for you?"

As I walked up the steep hill of my long driveway after lunch, the unmistakable body-rush of the ecstatic presence came through, surrounding and holding me motionless in my tracks for several seconds. Waves of ecstasy engulfed me entirely.

Vea's presence was potent, as it always is out in the woods, and I laugh out loud at the charismatic power of my companion, who has won my attention, devotion and affection.

Looking back, I remember feeling that strong force imploring me to leave that last relationship. Beckoning in the wee hours as the mortal lay sleeping beside me with whispers of a mission that did not include him but required ME fully.

I am finally aligned with my authentic self, in my own space, feeling the exuberance of freedom.

3 April

During my run today I received this:

"Study Spanish...create healing space on island...soon you will feel your sparkle...your presence will be uplifting...you will awaken higher consciousness in all whom meet you...have clear mind be your medicine."

4 April

These pages catch the flow of my fresh, morning mind when unhindered and mostly quiet, and the incessant racing of it is calmer these days. Morning tea finds me serene & grateful in my delicious solitude. My girls are happy, healthy and awakened to their own spirit. My assignment has been successful as a parent/coach to these two children. The 'job' is not done, per se, as awakening God's love in all hearts I meet is in effect as long as I walk in this body.

Woodpeckers are out in force and their calls occupy trees all around. Started running again, and feeling more alive, awake, refreshed and enthused because of this.

Purchased a machete and a titanium ring with 7 tiny diamonds. The symbology spoke to me- - 7 diamonds representing the letters of my new name, Guevara, and titanium being the strongest metal. The machete, well, it's time to keep my island cleared of the blackberry bush brambles as they shoot up again and again, I *will* keep that island cleared of brush my *self*.

I love my machete. The energy exerted in its use is therapeutic for my mind and good strengthener for my arms. Any frustration I've ever had can be directed into whacking the pestiferous brambles, completing the job quickly and making it more fun. I sometimes put names on the targets as I slam my machete through their root systems, weeding them off my island and out of my life.

9 April
Early Morning

<u>DREAM:</u> Che and computer room intrigue. A passport with a different identity came through for me via a fax machine, including the blue cover. There were many hallways and many official looking men in suits from whom I had to be on guard. I was amidst 'the enemy' in offices, not as soldiers in the jungle. I was shown pictures of Che and his children and was helping him somehow. We clearly spoke and I loved him in the dream. He had a darker complexion and was barrel-chested. His appreciation of me was palatable. We spoke over some device and I saw him on a screen monitor walking down and through office hallways wearing a white business shirt. The scene shifted to a beach where he wore a flowing white shirt, not revolutionary fatigues. He spoke to me from the 'other side' of the veil between our worlds.

10 April

Receiving direct and clear communications from Vea to publish these diaries detailing our union, and I am emphatically hesitant about doing this. No way do I want public judgment on the state of my mental faculties or the validity of this life-changing event to be up for the ignorant public to dispute, ridicule or invalidate. To come out with a story this abstract could surely find me in a vulnerable position. This situation is VERY personal to me, very private, and to go public with this is an extremely scary thought when I resist trust of my inspiration. I've judged it enough myself!!! **It's MY very personal experience.**

11 April

On the phone, Neal asks me to share my experiences of this multi-dimensional union, but it is difficult explaining a communication and communion that at best can be described as telepathic. It is impossible to explain to anyone this knock-my-socks-off *relationship* I am experiencing with an *invisible being*.

Pure bouts of Divine love--sounds cliché, but being enraptured in ecstasy is a very real experience for me defying explanation. Vea gives me this experience just walking up the road or performing a mindless task at work, always at random times. When he springs it on me, whatever earthly endeavor I am involved with is irrelevant.

There is a difference in Vea's presence and communication from that of the guides I have known since childhood. There is no confusing this. Again today is the persistent communication that he wants me to
"come out with this very soon".

I must meditate on this as I write these words. There is something sacred about this time and space without anyone outside my inner circle knowing. But then again it feels good to follow my heart, publish this amazing experience, and trust that whoever needs to read this book will. Don't fear anyone's opinions, they don't matter anyway.

✼ MY UNLIKELY UNION EXPANDS ✼

12 April

My morning meditation is a centering way to begin each day since I never know what to expect from this abstract union with my invisible companion.

I received the oddest request for something I've never done, been inclined to do or knew anything about...Vea asked that I perform what I've since learned is called "Rescue Work", for some of his comrades that "followed him to the death", assisting in their *release*. Intense heat rushed over my body breaking a sweat as I received this request.

Calling my friend Lori who has done this work with others, she reluctantly agreed to help from her house, as I was headstrong to do this with or without her. Her concern was with the possible effect it could have on me and she was annoyed at Vea for making this request. Having neither participated in or even hearing of such work, I was unaware it could have any adverse effects on me. Why would it anyway, my guides love me!

My inner adventurer awakened, I had no worries in this regard, and felt confident doing this work, evoking all the protection from the angelic realm and light-guides, placing myself in the sacred space of protection in my home. To me this was another adventure and I was curious about being involved with it. **I love my curiosity!**

It took two hours preparing myself for the thirty-minute task, and these details are of no intrinsic value for recall, hence their omission from this journal.

I had consulted JS, who is well acquainted with the invisible world as well as having worked on Vea and me. After the 'rescue' I rang him and upon *tuning in* he said, "your work freed only one, Che didn't have as many comrades as he thought he did."

14 April
Early morning

Today is the birthday of my first-born and I contemplate as my daughters both plan to conceive: would my ghost and his comrade each incarnate to one of my daughters thereby meeting again? Does it work that way? Hell, it works *any* way at all and ways *unimaginable* to the limited human mind. This whole experience has shown me *anything is possible*. There are probably more possibilities than we have numbers to count them. **I tell my ghost I'd rather not be his grandmother.**

Brandy's prayers for rain are answered on her birthday.

15 April
Sunday Morning

Warm tea and stoking of the fire have relieved my inner chill. I sit rocking in my chair with closed eyes and appreciation of the angelic presence, for all that I have, for all that I am receiving and for this new energetic, loving presence in my life...even though it wreaks havoc and I *can't see it*. Divine Providence (aka God, etc.) created bliss, humans created suffering. Obstacles are strengtheners, and not intended to be pits of prolonged suffering. Utilization of our empowerment creates perfect life, serene mind. My life is proof of this although I am not immune to bouts of depression's blackness and despair where bliss is only a dream. In those times, counting blessings doesn't alleviate suffering. I allow it to run its course as I remain open to receive the course of action. Tuning in to what thoughts make me feel better is like trying to run in a vat of molasses. Allowing it to run its course is to not resist it. Allow the darkness to be present and feel it without wallowing. Now there's a balancing act! Like childbirth contractions, resisting makes it hurt more, to breath with it and allow it is to work with it and it will pass sooner. Without these contrasts of the darkness and despair, one would lose sight of the joyousness when lightness of spirit returns.

Sounds like I'm in a rainforest with the songs of so many different birds.

This Che thing has really altered me, or shall I say, I have really grown and changed within this cocoon of another dimension that I share with what I have come to call amongst other things, "my ghost."

Where *is* my ghost anyway? His comrade buddy is freed up and now he seems gone again. My old fears of abandonment kick in. Human yearnings stir for Vea's uninterrupted presence, not for mortal romance. Frustration envelopes me realizing myself still so vulnerable to yearnings and abandonment issues even after receiving so much incredible guidance from my invisibles. Constant companionship with a being in another dimension is an unreasonable desire and simply not something I should focus on 'having'. To focus on what I feel I don't have gives momentum to the illusion of being abandoned and separate. There is no separation-only my fear of it.

Is yearning for adventure a preferred human condition to longing for a mortal lover? No yearning for anything is preferred! What about all the other dimensions? Would they make the pyramids, Paris, Iguazu, Venice and all the earth's wonders pale by comparison?? Probably. Who knows?? Maybe I should lighten up and be more playful with all this AND with being ME in this most unlikely union. **It is quite a colorful and a grand adventure after all!!!**

21 April

I love the new name signifying my rebirth in Argentina. The birthing process *of me* these past two years has been an extremely painful and difficult transition. Any birthing process has intense contractions, though, and this one is no exception. Not resisting is the key. The challenging times of the integration of this invisible companion are not over, but I do feel more aligned with the process.

The absence of his presence currently bestows some relief, compared to the programmed abandonment issues. But never knowing what's next finds me skating the thin ice of anxiety in worn old skates with edgeless blades.

Walking outside last night I felt the familiar ominous, energetic intensity, stalking me as a mountain lion stalks his prey, reminiscent of the early days of his perceived invasion of my space. I feel his 'frustration' at my continued bouts of skepticism. He makes it known he's not only frustrated with it but 'getting bored' that I've lost my steam with the momentum of our union. "Wanting a *real* sign" mentality does not suit him (or me!), and whenever it creeps up on me, I hear his consistent reply:

"Isn't Ave and Vea enough? ... play with those sounds, how they intertwine, how you came to even **know** them!"

I rebuke all doubt when I receive this, and give my trust over to the situation once again. It just gets *too consuming*! And I hear as I write this:

"There's a message in the consumption...
... go with it and trust!"

He's right there *in my mind* replying to my thoughts before they are even fully surfaced, when they are still 'pre-thoughts'! How cool is that???

22 April

DREAM: The ultimate chase and hide. I was in an army and the army had sentenced me to die. No trial, nothing, just death.

I escaped and went to family, which were my girls. Only my girls & I were present. I was at our home strategizing my escape when it hit me in a flash that they'd come and interrogate my girls. I felt a wave of panic. I was planning on writing about the position of being wanted, facing death and being innocent of the charges against me.

We decided to 'duck into the darkness of a cinema'. There I told them, "everything is in the bottom drawer, and I must leave you as my capture is imminent."

The scene switched to me with my friend Callaway. He had the usual cool and calm demeanor as his real life character. I was wearing a black trench raincoat. It was very billowy with an exaggerated amount of fabric from the waist down. We were driving in his van when we realized I needed a disguise. They would be looking everywhere in my hometown so we decided I should go to Mexico and never return.

The scene suddenly switched and I was in front of a firing squad. I was telling them emphatically, "Just shoot point blank, close up to my head or the back of my neck". I didn't want to experience the impact of a far-range shot.

The dream ended at me scurrying about and it seems the captors were everywhere. My clothes were baggy, messy and my hair had been newly shorn.

I awakened in a panic, literally out of breath from a space of pleading for more time so I could write. I don't remember the actual capture, but the memory of that persists very strongly.

Was I reliving Vea's experience as Che having been captured or that of the many victims of his revolutionary activity, both or none of the above?

*   *   *

. . . later . . .

"stop writing...stop writing, just <u>be with me</u>!!!"

I hear this loud & clear as I look for my journal, which was in my bed.

"be quiet...be still, just *be* with me, feel this!"

That dream re-aligned my core with Vea. I feel him urging me to be grounded and focused on our work, not skeptical and doubting my sanity or blaming imagination at fabricating his presence. He further communicates my habit of dependence on him is

"getting in the way".

Even as I tune into That Which Created All, I receive an almost identical message from *our* guides (the guides I've known since childhood are not the same beings after Vea's presence was integrated)

"Ave & Vea were joined...to doubt this and further apply THE ENTIRE spectrum of issues attached to fear is truly blocking the next vital step to your own success...
F-O-C-U-S"

"Minimal telephone conversations, no more long conversations with others...all work **is** the play...
"be joyful in the focus... wear a watch and love it, embrace it...being tired and giving in to worldly distractions is fear based and blocking you from the divine play...no, Vea is not to be one of your grandchildren...he will not incarnate through your daughters or anyone right now...he is your resonant companion, your partner...you have expansion to play with and enjoy and simply "be with". There's nothing "to do" or accomplish. Learn to simply allow this. You and he are one. Surrender to it and trust in this gift...

You are his beacon for the navigation his soul currently needs that is beyond human understanding."

With minimal morning grooming--only brushing teeth to not disturb residual energy from the dream still lingering so strongly, I decided to go for an early walk. As I steal a quick glance passing the mirror, I notice my reflection held the look of Che's face from his Bolivian capture superimposed on my own. His energy feels woven with the fibers of mine. We are not separate.

This is a 'potent' day, first the dream and then the communications received. I was moved to pick up my guitar and play "Ascension", the English/Spanish song I've written. Springing from my voice, the melodious language came forth with the natural flow of one who speaks fluent Spanish.

★ LIFE IN THE HOUSE OF SPIRIT ★

<u>23 April</u>
<u>12:05 A.M.</u>

A sense of urgency came through with the 'instruction' to be more present with Vea, spending less time talking with the earthly friends. So now I am required to be a hermit???

Developing a new signature for a new name is an activity I enjoy, especially with the *entire* name changing. After much practice, I've come up with what feels in alignment with my inner artist.

<u>Same day ... 7 A.M.</u>

Serenity of mind happens when I trust Vea's presence has been orchestrated by simple resonance of our frequencies for the specific purpose of spiritual expansion, not from some fantasy of a past life love relationship. It is not *personal* although my personal evolution and life circumstances found me to be the one standing 'closest to the door when it opened'. My human-ness would *like* it to be personal, but reality dictates this may not be so. I still have a hard time accepting **THIS** aspect, and ride that emotional roller coaster when I'm not aligned with acceptance. Sometimes though, there is an affection between us that is difficult to believe is not essentially *personal* by human definition. I feel affection and a deep connection of love with my unseen companion.

Outside in the rain today cleaning the dead wood out of a little berry-thicket cove by the creek, I received some messages:

"landscape what you've already got.
less phone talk, more Vea. more silence.
more focus. creative endeavor work."

The communication that I'm repeatedly receiving warrants my immediate adherence to the content.

24 April

Lesson 151 in ACIM speaks with me directly. ✦ I am resurrect*ing* my liberation. The mortal men with whom I've been involved had dysfunctional habits and minimal to no desire for spiritual exploration, making me glad to be in union with a non-mortal being (even if it **does** kick my ass sometimes!). The judgments I have of his past incarnation activity come and go. It is my personal growth at play involving judgments of *any kind*, hence, a characteristic of the 'Holy Relationship'.

Joined by Divine Providence, the intent of an earthly marriage is a *reflection* of the gift the Holy Relationship provides. The couple is to use the vehicle of their union to grow within their own selves ever closer to their Divine Nature and expand the love that is shared out to others.

✦ *ACIM (A Course In Miracles) Lesson 151—excerpts that 'speak to me': All things are echoes of the Voice for God.*

No one can judge on partial evidence. That is not judgment. It is merely an opinion based on ignorance and doubt.

You do not seem to doubt the world you see. You do not really question what is shown you through the body's eyes. Nor do you ask why you believe it, even though you learned a long while since your senses do deceive.

How can you judge? Your judgment rests upon the witness that your senses offer you. Yet witness never falser was than this."

30 April

My invisible guides emphatically instructed me to maximize my nutritional intake. My body is in dyer need of the nutritional ammunition required to continue running the intense energy of this union without burning up my nervous system. I tend to not eat much, but when I do, it's healthy food, organically grown fruits, veggies and gourmet cheeses with gourmet crackers, and I'm not big on food prep and making myself actual meals.

... 9:00 P.M.

Processing many human emotions from feeling Vea's absence...anger, sadness and the full spectrum of ego-based illusory mind fucks.
In witnessing my emotional upheaval, I feel like a whiney child immersed in a tantrum of disempowerment and separation from the Source.
Ah, the ups and downs of a partnership from out of this world!

01 May

My emotions are all over the map. I'm sure the upcoming wedding has a hand in this along with some emotional effects at the upcoming presence of my daughter's long-absent biological father. He has never contributed anything but the pain of his absence to the psyche of this innocent child growing up. And now he wants to come to her wedding?????

I do not feel Vea's presence. His absence activates the old dragon of human longing. I work at shifting any mind activity in this regard so to not nurture self-deception. Need to clear my mind fully and observe this dragon at play rather than put forth the energy it takes attempting the perceived slaying of it. I must simply allow it to be and just pass through rather than wage the war of resistance that cannot result in victory.

I received a communication from what seemed like a *deeper dimension* than previous transmissions:

"Presence is about attention, intention and focus.

Currently my attention is working with events in Cuba and forces pertaining to this arena. My attention is DIVERTED; hence you do not feel my presence. We have our work and we have work that seems separate to you now. You must be patient with timing and other factors you do not comprehend with your limited human faculties.

Continue to do your work and allow the shifts to happen without getting caught in the trap of fears, desires, attachments and other emotional blocks. I am not limited to being in one space.

Our connection is established. Know this and trust, put trust above all else and allow your work to flow tirelessly. Ease up and trust all is well."

<u>3 May</u>
<u>Early morning</u>

My home is THE HOUSE OF SPIRIT permeating with silence and delicious stillness. Bird songs herald in the morning after yesterday's downpour had them all silent. **This is the home of Vea and Ave, the working headquarters of a transformational union.**

<u>DREAM</u>: (fading) I had medical issues regarding the brain and was with a group of others with a similar condition. Medical personnel administered jolts with an electrical shocking device. It hurt like hell and melted the neck of a guitar I was holding. I felt completely helpless at the mercy of these cruel people who seemed to derive pleasure at hurting us.

★ LEGALIZATION OF AVE ★

<u>4 Mayo</u>
<u>... 7 A.M.</u>

I awaken from a yummy sleep in crisp, clean linens with a warm fire to the sound of drizzling rain. I am enveloped in the epitome of coziness this last morning waking up officially as
Kari Denise de Velasco

WELCOME...Ave Guevara de Velasco!
Today is my own private celebration day.

Last night's music session alone in my cabin, I played 'Ave Maria' on my violin for hours, then with my guitar, I sang my song in beautiful flowing Spanish finishing off my session with some renditions of Hank Williams, 'I'm So Lonesome I Could Cry'. I feel aligned with supreme personal success along with being so lonesome I could cry, and did so.

<u>...11:11 P.M.</u>

Today the courts granted me legalization of my new name. Ave Guevara de Velasco is officially born into the world.

Cinco de Mayo

It's a personal, solitary transition from Kari to Ave. Couldn't have picked a better date for my re-birth. The Universe (working through the court system) orchestrated the perfect timing!

☆ EVICTING THE GHOST ☆

6 Mayo

My companion returned. I am *told* that *"mum's the word"* on his return, not to discuss it with the family or anyone.

Major shift is occurring. Silence is required of me. No phone talks. If it *is* Vea, the energy feels *way* different. It is to be between US ONLY. He says lovingly yet with firmness that I must work on my dependence of him as he works on his rage.

"Our union will heal this for each of us."

I have a strong wave of fatigue and repulsion desiring only peace, which this association does not provide on any consistent basis. I want the part of me back that never *heard* of Che Guevara! I announce out loud for the invisibles to *HEAR*:

"Vea, it's been *great*, and we shared on major levels of profound experience. Whatever is the Will of The Creator is my will *only*." I no longer crave the energy or presence of whoever you are. "My divine source alone will do *just fine*. No other cravings, they are only distractions from my journey back to the Source of my Divine Nature. I WILL NOT write a book and offer this wild ride up for public consumption. *I hereby release whoever you are, whoever my ghost has been.*"

I feel strangely free. I've never 'broken up'
with a ghost before.

⋆ LIONS, VEA & WALK-INS ⋆

7 May
7 A.M.

I'm in some form of personal heaven feeling up close and
personal to the angelic realm, like the veil between the worlds
has lifted. Vea returned feeling *very* differently, very
peaceful. Silence reigns between us. No intrusive energy or
'instructions', just *feeling* him. Just *being*. It's soft,
affectionate and calm as we just sit within each other. It's
awesome and calming.

Took a walk last night just before dark. I love my family
compound, and being outside soothes any weariness of spirit.
The abrasive feeling of my multi-dimensional companion has
smoothed out. *He simply will not go away.* I surrender
to this love from out of this world.

10 May

The wedding of my precious Amelya is next weekend. My
baby will be a wife!

Went to sleep last night to the sounds of two mountain lions
communicating. Wild, beautiful, intriguing.

...11 P.M.

The screams of the mountain lions are again resonating
throughout the woods right now. Their unmistakable
screams had enough distance between them for me to detect
their two beings communicating.

Since Vea's gentle return two days ago, he feels completely gone again. My lack of understanding of the purpose of these comings and goings shakes me up but seems to be the nature of this union. From fulfillment of his presence to the void of his absence, I must make peace with this and heed all the communications I've received. My attachment to the gift being with me full time is the cause of my difficulty. I am on a roller coaster of acceptance and oneness and fear of separation and resisting 'what is'. I haven't allowed the feeling of joy to grow from this energetic love integration. Too much fear is stifling the momentum.

<u>**13 May**</u>
<u>**1 A.M.**</u>

The wedding rapidly approaches.

The mountain lion again screams in the canyon *next to my cabin.* **Wonderful, powerful, I love this wild life!**

Channeled experience during my walk:

Feeling the 'bubble containing us all". Everyone is a particle that floats, 'bumping into' and/or merging with others. Their movement continues to either keep going *through* each other or join together for periods of time for cycles of learning. The bubble has a thick, gelatinous consistency and I **see *it*** - a brilliant blue. This interconnectedness revealed itself 'graphically' on my morning walk.

Communion with Spirit feels light and refreshing, and during this communion the unmistakable presence of Vea immerses me in extended ecstasy. **He's *back*.**

* * *

Listening to my tango CD's brought home from Buenos Aires carries me back to that world. The culture merges with me and I feel gifted to have it colour my life. Playing my violin most nights, a new level of sensuous is morphing up from within Ave. Playing tango on this glorious instrument transports me through a passage between worlds.

I read about 'walk-ins' and how in the 'paranormal' realm this can and does occur. I've been researching online in an attempt to uncover similar events to what I'm experiencing with Vea. As he *won't go away*, I am compelled to gain a logical understanding of this most illogical situation. This association has its most pleasant side effects, but it's also unnerving. I've read all about medium-ship, automatic writing, walk-ins, and the like. I have found nothing that comes close to defining the situation that has become my life.

I've entertained fantasies of Vea 'walking-in' to someone and appearing at my door looking quite like Zorro in that black cape, painfully handsome and mysterious, proclaiming in that sexy Latino accent **"I AM VEA".** I've earned the right to entertain a sense of humor about this.

Upon my walk this morning, just before the beautiful vision of the blue sphere containing all creation, I heard these words in no uncertain terms:

"<u>YOU ARE</u> THE WALK-IN.
   STOP LOOKING OUTSIDE YOURSELF FOR ANYTHING.
EVERYTHING YOU WILL EVER NEED IS RIGHT WITHIN YOU."

I will never forget how 'hearing' that phrase so clearly felt throughout my *entire* body, even though it sounds like one of those lines that have been *so* overdone in all those spiritual self-help books (except for the *walk-in* part). Hosting a 'walk-in' and being alive and still conscious of this has not even been remotely referred to as anyone's experience I've read about so far.

It was 'explained' to me the error in looking outside myself for anything:

"It's a human condition."

This clears up some confusion and anxiety over my continued lack of understanding. I felt pressure from outside myself pushing *onto* me, and heard:

"GET IT! You're on the VERGE!"

I wonder how many humans have been engaged in this identical activity, whether they hosted a former earthly icon or not. The power of this engagement actually evoked a name change. My premonition of a transition in Argentina that would change the course of my life, sensing a rebirth and a renaming turned out to be accurate given the outcome of this event. Having had previous premonitions and communications throughout my life that have come to pass exactly as I had *received* them, proved to me again the authenticity of this experience.

Upon his return this week, it was gently explained to me that he never left; my own fear of loss activating the grief process was instrumental in clearing this human programming.

"Your fears are the ultimate coyote. Humans have a thick screen clouding themselves from clarity and vision...they have no idea or acceptance of the possibilities to be experienced in their lifetimes...walk-in's, as you call them, don't just happen to the dying, dead or insane.

We are advising you to not again indulge in grieving the loss of something not lose-able, but to keep the flag out for soul recognition when he returns from his perceived departure as he experiences the other side with new freedom. He is playing with his liberation. When you feel that intense love rushing through your being, he's occupying your common space. Do not share this information with anyone for several days...this must integrate with your consciousness."

(Note: The 'flag to be kept out' is my love, awareness and trust for this union and Vea himself. As this communication was received, knowledge came in with it of the flag's meaning: *it is a light for him to be drawn back through the matrix of the layers of dimensional fields)*

"Vea has been awaiting the readiness for the resonant being on Earth for the purpose of his continued evolutionary work"...your recognition of him took place when you 'met him' in Argentina because you were ready for this union and the work it would require on your behalf to accept this...both parties have to be ready for the conscious union of this nature. The western mind finds this foreign and calls this situation illness, the ancient shamanic mind, attuned with the unseen world knows well this 'condition' is the birth of a healer, a bridge between the worlds."

"Ave is the female counterpart of Vea. Your recognition of, and courage to change your resonant sound (name) to what was directed, indicates to the host of invisibles you understand and accept this union, you are the one that resonates completely for the entirety of this expansion. The timing of your arrival in Argentina was the confirming factor of your absolute readiness. You are expanding to hold the space to 'be' a bridge between the world of matter and the world of spirit—it is all energy of differing frequencies."

"He is yet attuned vibrationally with 'Guevara', and his desire is for you to be attuned with this sound. This is a union (marriage) of two energies attuning with a shift greater than that of each individually. The name is a tool you have been given to assist with this shift that you and he are aligned with in your expansive healing work. It is not only a symbol for you of this union, but it IS the name that joins you on the earth plane. You ARE Guevara, and this can be a difficult passage for you during your resistance, but you will come to trust in your essence, what you are receiving, and you will find ease with the allowance of your personal expansion through these non physical avenues of communication that seem foreign to the human experience."

"The term 'marriage' differs significantly from the definition and imposed limitations of earthly marriage."

14 May

Vea is Ave's male counterpart--I AM the 'walk in'. Although the term WALK-IN was used in the telepathic communication I received, mine is not the same experience as the definition I found in my research. I believe they used that term with me because it was the closest thing I could understand to what they were communicating, and they knew I could relate to it.

It doesn't matter what it's called, *it's happening*! Having the term only provides comfort for the sake of the human in this relationship (me).

Are not our bodies temporary housing for our *spirits* 'use' in realizing our divine function in this dream we call life? So why wouldn't we share our bodily vehicles with partner spirits? The belief of one body having one spirit within it is another close-minded, limitation we set upon ourselves. Society has mental illness terms and scores of medications for anyone who has experienced this, yes? Trust, clarity & perseverance are the only medicines to assist with the success involving a situation such as this.

I am adamantly closed to intimate relations with any mortals (or any other *spirits* for that matter!). I am fulfilled enjoying this body and the solitary lifestyle doing this work from the direction I've been given. Prayer, meditation and staying awake are essential.

"Aloneness and fulfillment are human conditions set upon themselves by choice of limited mind use. However, the state of fulfillment accommodates the human to be of maximum service without distractions, as is being in a body not riddled with physical pain/mental anguish. Illness and pain are either profound teachers or absolute distractions depending on the choice of the host. The continued anguish you experience from this shift is from the societal programming that disconnects humans from spirit. As you are awakening to this vital connection, the programming is dissolving and expansion is occupying that energetic 'space' within your cellular composition. Your natural response is to resist this and label it with those terms inherent in the programming, thus creating great fear and further resistance. The upheavals bombarding your mind are dissolving the programs and opening the aspect you perceive as self to the fullness of its being and the field of infinite possibilities that are within your realm of creative empowerment, wired into the soul, but disconnected from itself due to human generations of programming from fear based limited minds under the illusion of separation from Source. You are reconnecting to the world of spirit as you have resonated with this to a greater capacity than acceptance of the societal belief systems imposed upon you since your arrival this lifetime. You came in to this life not resonating with what you heard or saw around you, and that resonance gained enough momentum to bring you to this reconnection and expansion.

This is why we want you Ave, to attain optimal physical condition through arming your body with maximum nutrition to support this spiritual/electrical/cellular shift."

17 May

The more I deny that which has always distracted me from truth and come to understand truth is just behind the veil of illusion, the deeper I merge into this union with Vea and understand why it came to be.

This union also brings me closer with Source, the Creator, as Vea is a facet of these and within it as am I, and it is only through my communion with Source that keeps me centered in my own Divine nature and free from earthly fear-based distractions. This includes the distractions that have been entirely consuming, resisting this union, this alignment with another aspect of the Divine's creation and my own spiritual awakening.

My unlikely union is simply with a being from a parallel dimension in the Divine play. Our interaction carries the same holy implications as a union between two mortals on the earthly dimension of existence. Any union can serve to distract or bring closer to God/Source those joined by the forces of Creation. (Let it be known, I do not think the Creator is either male or female!) This work takes constant focus and prayer.

21 May
Monday morning

Woke up from a nightmare of being shot at and barely escaping with my life and the lives of the children I was attempting to save.

I'm sporting a lively headache from the bit of champagne I had toward the end of the evening of the perfect wedding day. Walking my daughter up the aisle was a delightful reward for the many challenges of the single parent experience.

⋆ ILLUSIONS OF SEPARATION ⋆

22 May

A cup of Earl Grey accompanies the *flow of quiet* as I retreat within, attempting to retrieve my energy back into the garment of my body/mind. Wrapped in my robe, the total emptiness that engulfed me after the wedding has been frightening despite all my experience and learning. Did I fall off the path into the blackened abyss of fear and pain from unrequited past love? The wedding stirred up everything emotionally dark from my depths to be healed under the beacon of awareness and letting go.

I have certain comfort with the level of emptiness that has shifted forth now that the terror of it has passed.

26 May

I practice holding the space of non-judgment that's either bad *or good*. This practice is a full time occupation, to just allow the pendulum of duality to cease movement altogether and be joyous without zestful enthusiasm that can turn to darkness in a moment. To hold this space takes constant effort, and even with applied vigilance I cannot hold it very long.

Joyousness is subtle yet *can* be held, and I've not yet been able to hold this state consistently. I lack momentum. A state of being to *hold*, not *cling* to and therefore lose grasp of. No grasping.

Holding contains no fear.
Grasping is fear based.

This "walk-in" mergence/transference is being consciously integrated. It is intense and *kicks my ass*, but it clarifies those 'mysteries' upon which I wondered throughout my life – with the present. **This connects the dots.**
Confusion and disorientation with my own identity and personality regarding the integrative shift and how to deal with its intensity is becoming clear and assisting me with being calm.

There is a level of difficulty in writing about this after the direction to publish. I feel a resistance to disclose details in the uninhibited way I wrote these notes before this was revealed to me.

Clarity and understanding are welcome soul-healing balm after the rough edged rollercoaster ride this past week AGAIN, accepting of the validity of this integration. So much makes sense now after the long period of searching and questioning, I have been illuminated with strength and courage. Trusting & feeling ease when I allow trust.

It's a mergence of energies, not a transference, although the entity and personality undergo a pseudo-transfer when mergence occurs, including the week before and after the occurrence. Maybe the change is just me expanding with it. It's all good when I allow myself to feel EASE!

29 May

I have flashes of *needing winter*, which is the approaching season in Argentina. I'm craving it, actually, missing 'my' country, yearning for that language. 'Stuck in English,' and the mediocrity of American society which lacks elegance, feels claustrophobic. Money is the focus in this country, not LIFE, working, not LIVING.

I'm partially caught in the trap enough to feel the pressure and see the ugliness. Ugliness being further judgment, hence the pendulum swings again. This motion does not allow my inner peace to be maintained. Most of me is elsewhere: Argentina, Brasil, Tuscany, Venice, *Iguazu*!
Can I just choose to NOT look at the ugliness, or do I just not give it any energy and look for the beauty in anything and everything?

2 June

"Darkness is Vea's journey" - Charlotte the healing facilitator tells me during a session with her to balance my energy field.

Am I on that journey **with** him?

The 'darkness' element evoking fear in humans doesn't scare me.
If I am part of this journey with my non-physical companion to assist with his expansion to the lighter part of himself, then I accept this with no fear, as I feel love with this. I give him all my light through love. The statement, "Through love, anything is possible" is being taken to a new level of experience of what we humans think love actually IS. Darkness is just light's contrast, without it, we wouldn't know the light when we see or feel it, so in essence, darkness is not to be feared, but faced with eyes that see its beauty.

I receive this brief and clear statement from my invisible friend:

"Human definition of darkness differs
from what darkness really is."

Moments of ecstasy revert to insane bouts of overwhelm within moments of each other. The integrative process is turning me inside out! This in turn makes me look at the state of being turned 'inside out' from a perspective that is different from the negative opinion of it that is programmed into all of us. To be turned inside out is so feared and resisted at all costs, that to experience it is truly a challenge to embrace.

What's the worst that can happen to me if I "go with the flow" of this sensation that is called inside out?

My affection for this non-physical companion and sense of adventure with this personal growth journey gives me the strength it takes to not have my nervous system fry with the increased electrical energy flowing through me. I exercise my free will as to how I react to this, and choose to put myself on a regimen of flower essence remedies that 'allow the light of understanding to transform discouragement and depression'.

I am called to assist my body with whatever will strengthen it to cope with these ongoing waves of havoc washing over me and through me, even with my acceptance of it. The integration process with my invisible partner directly affects me on a cellular level and on levels I didn't know existed within the human body/mind system.

Being turned inside out gives me a very detailed view of parts of me that I didn't even know I had, but have reacted to and created situations from my entire life. It's actually refreshing when I put down resisting and fearing it, and look at this as a journey of self expansion rather than from running that old program of what is "normal" – and if you're NOT what was programmed in as normal, then there's something wrong with you.

This whole experience is in my life as it is right now, because I've been awakened to what's RIGHT with me, thereby attracting this in the first place! I'm actually pretty cool, an official 'mystic' ~ the ones you read about that live in caves or forests, on remote mountaintops, which is the opposite of what everyone thought of me when I was a kid in school being bullied! For decades I lived my life believing what those bullies told me I was and as insignificant as my parents told me I was. This experience is dissolving all those old belief systems I held about myself that attracted the life of struggle that I'd always known. **This feels like a powerful shamanic transformation!!! No wonder it's blowing my mind!**

I'm experiencing a multitude of memories that were extremely painful regarding my years as a single mom. Rejection, abandonment, poverty and constant struggle were common threads throughout my life. The past is regurgitating to be healed, not re-lived; truly, my cellular structure is experiencing purification. I am expanding beyond those memories, dissolving my identification with them. **This is what being liberated feels like!!!**

I always took solace in knowing whatever my situation was, it could be worse, and it can always get better. I raised my girls stating this at least once a day all our years together. Knowing persistent self-work while imagining how a better situation would FEEL was exercising my choice to attract better life circumstances.

I lived this as the example to pass on to my children. I knew how I lived, more than what I said was the most important of life lessons to give a child. This recitation followed by having one's occupation be something you love and are passionate about broadens limiting belief systems about working and following ones dreams, warding off the destructive habit of self-pity and living an unfulfilled life. I always believed I could live the life of my dreams and taught my daughters that they could too, and they must indeed discover what it is that stirs their hearts, that ignites what is known as passion.

Looking at earth from space, I realized all of us were just microscopic specks of life.
Having this realization, rather than feel like an insignificant speck, I decided I was going to be a BRIGHT speck!!!

This current experience, when I don't resist it, is turning up the wattage of my inner light. THIS I know for sure!

6 June

Simplicity beckons from the throes of a black pit depression since the wedding. Does this darkness herald in a new phase of life, cleansing out the official 'role of mother' with my baby taking a husband? My priority shifts are changing, as I have 'no interest' with pursuing success and notoriety with my music, but to simply enjoy the expression of it. I've harbored a dream of success with this for as long as I can remember. To *hell* with that industry, it's a rat race of commercialism and conformity. Music is a gift not to be exploited for money or the masses, and I refuse to participate in that madness or distract myself with the desire for it.

His presence just now returned as I write this, subtle but unmistakable. **My true love resides in another dimension.** There is nothing crazy about this; the craziness was in the loves I've known in **THIS** dimension!

Currently, this moment (as this transition requires living moment to moment) I don't trust any communication, as it could be self-deception. Yet, whenever I write or even think this way, I hear a gentle:

"She doesn't get it fully yet."

8 June
5:45 A.M.

DREAM: There were two huge groups of people, the assemblage felt theatrical. My 'group' had Che as leader. We wore red robes and were naked underneath. I was a white girl and we all had guns. I never saw him, but he was always there. Peripheral glimpses. I longed to see him as we had a connection separate from the group.

144

The dream's fading as I write this, but just before it ended, I was filled with the knowledge that I was the mother of Che. There was a little puppy. At one point my robe came off and I was naked, feeling vulnerable. A kind man, very tall, gently and respectfully re-robed me. We were outside beneath some structure made of wood with open sides. My extreme love for Che was prominent throughout the dream as was the longing to see him. People around me were speaking Spanish. I had a position of significance and was being looked after by some who were bilingual, as it was known I spoke only English.

19 June
Midnight

These are the last days of spring. It seems the creatures of the forest, just moments ago restless with their different sounds and footsteps outside my window, have settled into rest.

My focus is to consciously host my Divine nature. I still have human desires, but mostly for my ghost to simply have a body. (Big grin, sparkles in eye!) I have found the fulfilling of human yearnings have not been fulfilling at all. Why keep thoughts about those things any longer when they do not serve me? With the fury and intensity my invisible companion possesses that I have firsthand experienced, it's probably a *good* thing he is not currently *in* a body! **Even without a body, it has unquestionably strong testosterone levels and knows well the art of enchantment.**

I am in Holy Relationship with one not contained within a body. How perfect! Perfect for him also; to have a living human respect the reality of such an abstract and unbelievable situation and *allowing* it to be, for him to express himself and me be open and willing to receive it, and to accommodate his merging with me. To not love him as the icon his past was or has become, but to love *only what he is NOW*. **I am told without question I am the one in complete resonance to play with him on this.**

I have a 'hint' of the mission of this situation, but it has not yet fully taken root within my consciousness. I do know it's requiring me to pay attention, be clear, and stay strong with my spiritual nature. **This is no simple task and it's expanding me further than I thought possible.**

Beyond sharing limited perceptions in traditional intimate relationships in which humans engage, both he and I are free to experience *different realms* of our selves *through* each other. This has not previously occurred for me with anybody and I don't currently believe it is possible to have this exchange between two mortals no matter how deeply in love they may be. I did imagine throughout my life the bliss of truly merging with another and occupying the *same* body. **Sex never provided this mergence, and in comparison is a cheap imitation.**

Traditional relationships with their mixed bag of issues and misunderstandings are something I have intended to never settle for again. **There is nothing ordinary about this union or this experience that is occurring.**

Perhaps I *did* invite this situation without conscious intent. Resonance with the thought of this sort of love being *possible* is what drew this situation into my life. Another request granted in one of those ways we cannot possibly expect! **So are the Mysteries of Life.**

There is no finer a love to share my essence with on this level. I don't think it *possible* to share a love of this nature with any human being.

I feel light beaming from my eyes and every pore of my body. This euphoria in every cell of my being is making it hard to get to sleep!

25 Minutes Left of 'Midsummer'

A fire is burning in my woodstove, and it is a historic time of festivity throughout the lands from ancient times. My body is sore all over from the staining of my deck with 3 different shades of color. Staining work commenced until 10 PM. Vea's energy coursing through me all day had me altered in an ecstatic sense. He was indeed strong with and within me. His presence unmistakable, I'm deliciously exhausted.

21 June
Summer Solstice

A very deep thought form pervades me:

"Our resonance attracted each other and the love is pure."

I love my ghost!

22 June

Alone on the property with my family next door gone on vacation, I have morning tea on the deck and yell full throttle, **"VEA!!!"** Many times I make this call inside and outside my cabin, my intention to fill the space totally with his name, allowing myself to call to him at the top of my lungs. The sound reverberates throughout the woods and the creek canyon. Yelling this liberates me with a sense of total abandon. It feels therapeutic to YELL!!! When I reach my arms up and look skyward, I am filled with this:

"I am right here within you...there is no 'difference'...the difference and separation anxiety is a human misperception only...it does not exist except in the human mind encumbered by the limitation of beliefs and fears.
Humans are so accustomed to yearning they think they always must, and miss the *actual* reality of the connection with which we are all part. Their energies merge and co-exist within the boundaries of the flesh...boundaries BEING YET another human mis-perception.

Know I am inside you and you yearn it because you don't realize you have it right now in this instant. Yearning blocks you from the bliss you can know in this instant and all the instants that follow. This 'following' of more instants, be they of bliss or anything else, is another condition of the human experience of time—past or future...
And yes, Ave, you feel me and I fill your thought patterns because our energies occupy each other on a conscious level, and it extends beyond what you are familiar with and out of range of...you therefore have fears of being insane or imaginative...I am not from either of those places; that is human reaction to a profound shift.

You are shifting to this 'new' expansion that is not really new, just not familiar within human-mind-reaction-experience. 'Expansion' is the only literal form this level of existence can possibly describe for your human mind to grasp. This level of existence is also transitional…

No, No, No, you are NOT insane or over imaginative out of loneliness…or any reason you can conjure up within your limited mind use. Please GET THIS and do not spend any more 'time' NOT getting it. Don't subject yourself to continued suffering from this distortional✦ thought form."

✦ *This transmission was 'automatically' written without my manipulating it to be grammatically correct.*

28 June

I *could* say, "I don't know what came over me", but that would not be true. I know full well the influence for my decision to have a shotgun in the corner beside my bed. I keep the shells in the nightstand on the other side from the gun. I practiced lying down as if asleep and retrieving, loading and cocking the gun for a quick response. Drilling myself for preparedness, I have never had an interest in anything like this at all!

I sensed myself to be fully entertaining my invisible friend, his host clad in French lingerie grabbing a shotgun and doing the drill over and over. I got good at this and it was actually *fun.* I felt empowered and it was a luscious feeling, this blending of us. **It was very playful!**

My ghost *insisted* on me having this form of protection and knowing how to use it in an instant. I entertained the thought of protection for myself, but the 'former' me would have simply gotten a dog to bark a warning and surround myself in protective 'light'. A shotgun? I will never not have one now and I will never not surround myself in protective light either. I sense my ghost was just being playful.

29 June

Vea beckons to just BE and not write.

. . . later

The shift is settling in with me after the channeling from the 22nd. The energy from it has been with me since. Kestrel hawks 'raising hell' in the surrounding trees and the airspace around my cabin is filled with their communicative sounds. On different days, different birds fill the trees with their presence and the air with their sounds. I find this fascinating and LOVE living out in nature, feeling the cycles, the creatures, the flow!

1 July

I've been 'directed' without question to come out with this. Replacing fear of loss of his presence with empowerment from reviewing all the channeled communications is the right direction to aim myself.

Vea feels relaxed now that we can progress with our expansion, embraced by the union we've integrated. This day is a celebration of this shift completion. The following transmission fills me immediately:

"There will be other SHIFTS... this too is a transitional state."

When I contemplate the remote possibility of a human-to-human intimate relationship happening someday, I immediately receive this:

"You simply cannot have intimate involvement with a mortal and be involved in the relationship of this caliber with Vea simultaneously...can't even have a dog."

My reactive and barely formed thought to this transmission being, "oh *man*, not even a *dog???* Now that's a high price to pay!"—was immediately met with this:

"It only *seems* like a price to pay from human misperception...you are giving up nothing to be engaged in this union, because the family pet or a male to 'be with' IS a meaningless distraction to you at this point. You've had a variety of both in this incarnation and you have finally *got* it.

Don't slip and forget that you've gotten it and find yourself distracted yet again. Do not voluntarily, disguised as an unconscious act, pull the veil back over your vision and awareness in the name of human conditioning that means *nothing* in the big picture. You've come far on this journey, our momentum is a grand blessing and our healing a great gift!

Know you have persevered, working long, deep and hard, and have gained momentum in being awake. The veil is off, and it's you and *you*.

Your initiation was met by your choice of impeccable action and thought."

3 July
Midday

The feeling of 'being stuck' has always propelled me with working or plotting more productivity strategies.

This similar feeling today is from a different source. It is indicative of standing on the threshold of an internal shift. It's taken persistent work to integrate into my life and psyche **what the hell is going on here.** This is simply not an everyday occurrence. I've already tried ignoring it and rebuking it through prayer, it does not leave me alone for long. I go back and forth between accepting and allowing it and feeling the higher place within myself through it's being with me and I with him, and then swinging back to the fear-based part of myself that resists, questioning the whole matter. **This pendulum swing is tiresome!**

Life immersed in Spirit accompanied by Vea, doesn't get any better. The purpose of this feels stronger than any fears.

So then I receive this:

"The human pangs of unfulfilled yearning will be non-existent soon" - (they almost are now, as my 'shifted self' picks up momentum)

. . . and then this comes in:

"No need to currently travel or yearn for it, as now you will attract those cultures into your life and to this homestead. You will attract the adventures to places you resonate with, trust in the timing that all is perfect. Our integration is your current grand adventure."

4th of July

A deer walks among the trees below and the sound of the creek flow meandering in its winding course to the river finds the flow of my gratitude. Vea 'appears', time to put the pen down and just BE with this magnificent energy.

5 July

The holiday BBQ in the neighborhood home of my old friend Douglas yesterday afternoon found me occupied fully by my invisible companion. A spread of wonderful homemade food by all the neighbors provided the culinary delight for me personally that evokes the awakening of my ghost.

This time I felt him merging into me and was able to divert my eyes from anyone seeing them roll in that unmistakable bliss. Fortunately I wasn't engaged in conversation and ate way more food than I usually do, fully enjoying the ecstasy always bestowed upon me when I am sharing my self with him uninterrupted.

He's been constant on the surface of my consciousness and I'm enraptured with the bliss and love that I still cannot translate adequately into words. Of course, I continue to give this description one helluva shot!

I have felt him visit the wife and location of his last incarnation lately. It was the first time I was 'included' by being made aware of this, even though the details weren't revealed they are irrelevant. He's been working with energies in Cuba, I am told.

Sunset on my deck in the 'jungle'

I am being purged of the human longing to belong with another human. It keeps coming up because it is engrained deeply within the cellular structure of my human-ness. This yearning is evaporating slowly as time goes by in this union with which I am now immersed.

Vea! Vea! Vea! The invisible one fills me entirely and the ecstatic oneness of his presence takes over. Pen down...

* * *

Peachy-pink scattered high clouds in a light blue sky. These woods are glorious and it feels like I am in the middle of a jungle! Life on my deck and on this land is as good as it gets here on this planet.

A more opulent lifestyle would undo the sublime peace, serenity and simplicity. So would a boyfriend or a pesky puppy.

The scent of nature - - ahhhhh! Blue sky loses its colour to gray.

Even within my deepest gratitude and peace, overwhelm can still attack me in an instant. The cause of this, I am 'told' is that my nervous system is challenged in accommodating the electrical current of a being from another dimension. Although we are not 'wired' to do this, increased nutrition can assist the body with the accommodation, exercise is key and acceptance rather than this continued pendulum swing into doubt and resistance is mandatory.

The heat is turning to a breezy evening cool. I must paint. The canvas and oils beckon.

6 Julio

Painting the horse canvas last night was uplifting. All stresses of body and mind dissolve when immersed in painting. I get to travel into the realms of inspiration and creation, no airfare required, no passport, no waiting on lines.

This early morning's walk found me overcome with Che's grief for his favorite fallen comrades that were what he thought his most promising soldiers. It's a brief process, but it runs through this human system of mine nevertheless. On my walks I've processed for him many unresolved issues that were inherent in his last incarnation. The hunger, the thirst, the asthma, the family, the frustration with the ongoing suffering on this planet of the vulnerable, and the rage.

These things just 'pop up' into my consciousness and literally 'bubble out' energetically and pass through. I always feel his gratitude toward me for allowing this without questioning, fear or doubt. We are making progress.

☆ LIGHTNESS OF BEING ☆

7 Julio
8 P.M.

Writing this from a delicious state of sleepiness. My channel is always open when I'm alone and now I find it so, even in the company of others. **Life is calmer after that ass-kicking shift.**

(No Date:)

On my morning walk upon remote trails in my 'neighborhood came this:

"Study Spanish, tango, self-defense...learn use of the handgun...walk, run, train & strengthen...use trampoline daily...less talk with any and all friends.

Begin taking nutrients containing the purple color spectrum; adding into your regimen of the fruit and vegetable nutrients...complete The Pigeon Chronicles...do your paperwork diligently.

The training on this path is necessary upon which to direct your focus...the work is at hand and you are to be strengthened in mind and body to accommodate and manifest it without compromising your empowerment, but rather enhancing it, thereby expanding it.

You are not being tested, this is your term, you are being observed and are not alone with this, and it will be known when you are ready for the next level of experience.

You chose and lived a life of 'training' through life experiences to occupy this body multi-dimensionally...it being issued to accommodate 'AVEA', the morphic field combination who was born Ernesto Raphael Guevara de la Serna in what appears to be a long time ago -it isn't- and Kari Denise de Velasco.

The resonant sound you have attracted and assumed (new name) Ave Guevara de Velasco reflects 'interior' mergence completion.

It is the 'final' confirmation, in human terms, of your understanding of non-separation of the ego's theme of "I-ness". Your open mind and willingness throughout this incarnation to expand for the utilization of this healing work has attracted into your awareness the essence of the companion and the purpose of this alignment. It is currently perceived by you as HIS mission you are granting accommodation to, hence your continued perseverance for clarity of the sense of purpose you have carried throughout your lifetime. In actuality, this act of expansion is perceived as a mission, when in fact it is more of a 'purpose' for being. Your perception of it being "his mission" of which you are assisting is part of the human-male/female programmed role of the woman being the supporter of the 'husband' – the wife who has no purpose of her own other than to bear "his" children and assist "him with his work"... observe that your life attracted experiences henceforth that opposed directly this programmed limitation that was imposed upon women for millennia. The 'burning' of this program through your own life is part of the healing work for humanity that you have been consciously working with. It is all so much more than we can explain here at this time for your complete understanding. That is why TRUST is such a vital aspect for your ease with this. Your ease and trust are vital for your well-being with this enormous multi-cellular dimensional shift and expansion.

It is imperative your openness continue through the perceived difficulties that arise for you with this companion. Also be it known that this is a resonance, not an assignment. There is no great one out in the cosmos assigning partners to each other, the laws of resonance equate who attracts whom, and the dimensional residence of each energetic matrix matters not.

Be clear it is not your perception of YOU alone that you are involved with, but the energetic entity that occupied the revolutionary incarnation of 'Che Guevara' and continuance of divine work he was also part of, although he lost track of it in that lifetime and the ones you jointly experienced before these lifetimes. Your involvement within the entirety of this work pertains to the aspect of re-balance of energetic repercussions and redirection of global focus upon that incarnation. This is the aspect of what is called the 'mission' that involves the mergence of your energies and purpose. Redirection of global focus on the image that remains with the mostly forgotten message he stood for is a level of healing for humanity that cannot be explained yet to you, nor is it necessary. Trust and ease are your priorities at this time.

Involved with the energetic entity previously named 'Che' and the field of notoriety of that incarnation makes it more challenging to accept, both by you currently, and by the collective mind of the current population after publication of these notes. It is destined to stir energies up with the populace as it has with you yourself, Ave, thereby necessitating development of ongoing, unshakeable strength, courage and confidence in what you have learned from this information you have been receiving. But this stirring is the very nature of the expansion that will result and is necessary for it.

It is not 'up for global grabs' through commentary on this literary work what humans would term 'phenomenal'. It is not phenomenal except to their limited minds.

Currently, this is for you only, Ave. Our moments in the natural elements, these transmissions that you are receiving and writing cannot be accurately or completely described to satisfy the collective judgmental mindset of anyone reading these accounts. The purpose is not to bring satisfaction to or defend this work to any beings that resist their own expansion through any of the many channels through which infinite intelligence comes. Many choose to remain locked within their belief systems no matter the cost to their own soul's essence or joyful existence . . . that is why there is no 'time' anywhere but on your dimension, as they can take as many lifetimes coming forth as they choose for the expansion to occur that is eventual. It matters not, we love them anyway.

Allow, Ave, Allow.

It is truly momentous for your invisible hosts and guides on dimensions you cannot possibly fathom, when you 'get it' and allow. There is great love and support for you from those of us who have accompanied you on this thread of experience for time beyond your comprehension."

10 July
7:30 A.M.

Yesterday was a fabulous time with my beloved little granddaughter. She 'did my hair', danced as I played violin and we ate cherries. She rolled around on me as I lay on the floor, such fun tousling around with the little angel. On her walk home she blew me many kisses. Sometime later, she walked over with a complete dinner plate set up for me by her mother. **I took my meal on the deck with the blessing of knowing it gets no better than this.**

I have zero desire for romance where I used to court what I deemed a healthy interest.

Vea's presence currently exceeds any desires. This multidimensional experience completes my purpose, completes **me**. I learn more from it than from any mortal-to-mortal intimacy, and it satisfies my spirit beyond what any mortal has ever been capable of 'providing'.

I have uncovered the warrior's true state of being: happiness, independent of outside events or waves of human emotion or darkness...another glimpse of totality.

Hence, I am the rightful partner in a Holy Relationship for the spirit once embodied as the infamous Che Guevara. I do not fear or judge his darkness from that life or whatever darkness remains with his soul. Darkness is merely a different aspect on the spectrum of light. It is neither good nor bad in the big picture.

I have always known I was 'being trained for something big' when life presented me intense and ongoing challenges I had to work out alone. Having turned to Source for assistance through those times has fertilized me to accommodate this current situation that could threaten my sanity, nervous system, sense of well-being, or life itself.

Those times it appeared I was alone, I knew myself to be in the company of that which Created All, and felt guided.

* * *

Vea's presence feels DIVINE tonight.
I am bathed in an ecstatic energy and know that this is what LOVE feels like. Words cannot describe this experience, and although I document it as best I can, nothing can actually convey the *feeling*. I could not possibly conjure this up through my imagination.

Living with a love who is on another dimension is extraordinary and so very private. I am in a prolonged state of bliss and being within-love.

It's difficult for my human circuitry, so programmed by past disappointments and heartaches, to receive this gift and know that it is a gift and not that I've gone off the deep end.

The past evaporates and there is only NOW. Vea is settling in. I am settling in with him. It's been truly rough for each of us to work through this shift. The rough spot has lessened and acceptance has built some momentum. We will be able to move forward with this sacred work. This transition is quite personal despite the fact that I will have to share it eventually.

11 Julio
Still sleepy...

Freshly awakened from a nightmare, I write quickly before the memory and residual feeling fades:

DREAM: In a big house (mine), a large group of kids playing music in an orchestral setting invaded my space. Music too loud for me to be heard or effective in resolving the invasive situation.

Then the sky began turning orange and billowy. We were being bombed. Utter chaos. Huge wind from bombs blowing everybody. Thoughts of family---EMMA!!!! Helacious destruction. People coming through with guns. At one point I had to play dead as soldiers (not in uniform, more like terrorists) passed me. I remember arranging myself carefully to look dead. In utter terror, I lay dead still.

(Dream continued even in my half sleep) When bombing died down, Brandy came screaming, "WHERE'S EMMA?" I didn't know. The scene turned to invasion of home by thug-types proclaiming to have a search warrant. I was keeping them at bay as they hassled me. Place was in shambles. Then two very young men in a big, fancy truck all dressed up wearing cowboy hats, smelling strong of men's cologne, came up to me. They demanded I give them something they thought I had; something considered contraband by the raiding soldiers. I just told them, "GET OUT OF HERE!" One got out of the truck and reached into my space and retrieved what he thought was what he wanted. The terrorist thugs saw this and intercepted. I went to beat them to retrieve what they took and did so, and then threw it down the driveway and it rolled like a big wheel of cheese. The thug grabbed it before it rolled into the street. He saw the ring on my finger and exclaimed, "ah HA!" and as he was about to seize it, I told him it was fake and averted misfortune.

At this point, in all my stress, I was aware I was dreaming and remember thinking I could end this by waking up. I decided in my lucid dream state that I wanted it to continue to see what transpired. But, I woke up fully at this point.

* * *

12 July

Gone are the yearnings during perceived absences. Present is the adjustment from his constant presence. Shifted are the perceptions once held by me of society and humanity.

We are microscopic in the overall scheme. Holding my 'bright speck perspective" kept my attitude positive during the many years of struggle. I held a firm determination that my authentic purpose warranted the strength and perseverance being developed through those struggles. **My intuition proved correct.**

The realization of AVEA, the multidimensional being of which "I" constitute half and had this body created to 'house' has rendered me other than who Kari *was*.

When I was very little, I was way in tune with it, I remember this knowledge clearly in my being as a tiny child before even being able to speak. And I remember clearly spending much time in wonder of this thing called "I". It felt foreign to me to have this individual perception of the "I" awakened. Those babyhood and childhood memories are clear and now make perfect sense. My entire life, those memories had me wondering what they meant and determined to one day know. Now I know beyond the shadow of doubt.

13 July
Sunset

The first bite of dinner prepared and served by my friend Jane found my eyes rolling with the familiarity of Vea's culinary ecstatic presence. Unmistakably him, I keep this to myself and enjoy the meal more than I myself ever simply enjoy meals.

15 July

Rendered unable to sit or stand upright - - I'm hovering outside of my physical body unable to 'get back in'. The strength of my will to chronicle this event as it's happening overrides barely being able to write at all and I keep dropping the pen.

After an entire day of heavy yard work including rock, slate and dirt moving, pounding bender board stakes into the hard packed earth making pathways, I am covered in sweat soaked dirt and can't stand up long enough to even shower. I manage to crawl to the fridge to supplement my hunger with some fruit, hard cheese and crackers, valiantly attempting to retrieve a sense of grounding. I keep slipping in and out of states of semi-consciousness engulfed in a bodily weariness beyond anything familiar except for the weariness after labor and delivery of a baby.

A powerful vortex opened in the yard after I measured out its exact center point and to stand in it was not unlike standing at the threshold of some otherworldly portal. The Che aspect of Vea worked my body so hard today it was clearly not upon even my own strong motivation that this task was accomplished. Latino music serenaded me as I worked.

I've been hovering in and out of my body for over 4 hours now. **"Where's my wife to bring me food and tend to me???!"**

16 July

Yesterday my work reflected that of an enslaved laborer on my property, with barely a break and stopping only to drink water and take food.

Very much a Che day as he inhabited my body/mind for many hours.

I just lay down on the floor of my yurt attempting to retrieve myself fully. My valiant attempt failed, and my body remained covered with dirt, dust and sweat as I drifted outside my body unable to get to the shower.

Much rock and slate moving, large, heavy slates being placed and piled, stake pounding to hold bender board in place and an excessive effort of raking to move heavy mounds of dirt had me covered in sweat. This energetic level of labor was out of character for me to do since my earlier years before the challenge of my hand injuries. Moved the heavy rocks out of tall poison oak thickets to 'do my pathways and steps my own damn self'. Wasn't about to *pay some man* to do what I've been wanting to have done for so long, that I decided to do it myself, with a vengeance and a good pair of work gloves. A heavy macho attitude ran the show all day.

Very sore body. So sore it makes me laugh out loud. Laughing hurts too, but I don't care. My kitchen and bathroom are a muddy manly mess. I love it. Vea's 'Che' damn near forgot this body of ours is 52. As I write and think this, I receive:

" The body is in good shape and the years it has tolled upon it does not matter—it still works and is in great condition to work hard."

I was like a bull in a china shop during yesterday's work. I knocked to the floor a copper vessel holding wooden spoons in my kitchen scattering them everywhere. Then my sleeve caught and tossed the red goblet I frequently set out for Vea onto the floor and broke it in half.

*   *   *

Later that night...

Still sporting a sore body feels so good, so *worked*. The spirit of Vea's "Che" inhabiting my body accomplished a lot of hard-core work. He reminded me of my fitness and ability to perform such labor, years on the planet being irrelevant. He is more of a slave driver than I am!

Truly, the life and space of who I was before Argentina has merged totally with this new reality and I will never again be whom I thought I was. I feel no grief interpreting this as a loss, only blessed that I resonated with this amazing rendezvous that blew my expansion beyond this dimension, beyond any limiting human belief system.

My children might say someday after I depart this earth that I believed myself to be possessed by Che Guevara. Upon this passing thought form, I immediately receive:

"Beliefs are meaningless. This reality is **NOT** a belief system in action."

He clearly doesn't miss even a THOUGHT I have!

17 Julio

Ravens caw today, and yesterday were raucous in the surrounding trees. I consult my Animal Speak book when one of nature's creatures makes an obvious visit to me. Its reference to this animal medicine is: 'Very magical, Shape shifting, Past life work at hand'-- timely information with the experience on Sunday.
Today I feel just plain GOOD. No overwhelm, only calm and centered in my power. Feeling and maintaining this, I realize its rarity.
Interviewed a new doctor in Sacramento from Annemarie's referral. As she has always referred well, I heeded her advice to interview a new physician regarding the bouts of overwhelm I experience. Without disclosing details of my invisible inhabitant, she tells me this condition is well within the normal range, and even better than many, not to worry, that I'm really fine. She affirms my life is going 'as it should with my inner journey at this phase' of life. Confirmation from this lovely doctor eases my mind.

To be told by a licensed physician that I'm actually within the *'normal'* range of something leaves me speechless! Currently I couldn't feel within the parameters of normal for all the màte in Argentina! My 'normal' diagnosis is amusing.

I'm cultivating enrichment so in my transitional time we call death, I will be at peace and feel fine with the passing from this bodily cloak to whatever is next.

I'm in no hurry for this life's end, as I do not feel near enough to my graduation from the spiritual school that I attend, my grade probably only being kindergarten. The course I'm currently on though, feels like post-graduate school!

18 July

Summoned out of bed and outside to discover rain 'whispering' down and in the southern sky a full and brilliant rainbow. I took many photographs and my morning tea on the deck beneath my large umbrella feeling the Promise of Divine Power infused into me. As the calls of the ravens had spoken, there is magic in my life.

Skunk scent gently wafts to my nose. I shall sit and take this tea on my rocker outside and just BE with Vea, whom I feel strongly. My angelics are also present. And then they speak to me:

"We told you yesterday it would rain, you didn't believe us."

Clouds are rolling in. *My not believing 'them' illustrates an important lesson for me with trusting my instincts. The rainbow illustrated fully the message about trust upon seeing it.*

"Instincts are Divine energy and trusting them is imperative to create from this realm."

The rains fall heavier now and this information comes to me after receiving the above written message:

"Trust, trust, trust -- release all fears."

I am infused with the power of the Divine.

"The wealth you are to possess will come from your literary endeavors. Take the family to shrines and places of concentrated elemental power with intent to awaken more fully the divinity and empowerment within them and all lives you touch, especially with the grandchildren.

The mergence of you with your light being is complete: the morphic field of Vea, the former life of which you are aware, whose darkness was equal to your light has shifted with you. Through you he will experience and is experiencing his awakening. His era and environs had him ripe to make choices which were opposite from his divine nature and his notoriety came from his essence going into the darkest of human distractions. No judgment – all beings experience the realms of this at various stages of evolution toward the light. Through your integration with him, your personal growth will also continue to deepen exponentially – the two of you will grow light speed through your mergence as will your capacity to love.
His healing lay in the balancing of the contradictions he lived and influenced the populace by, you are assisting him with this balancing by your acceptance and allowance of this union, which seems unlikely only from the limited human standpoint. Spiritual awakening and feeling there no choice but to kill for a belief system, was followed by what he believed was betrayal. Following his continued hard work for a cause to which he abandoned his sense of self, he believed he lost everything to the one that betrayed him. Hatred and bitterness to forgiveness...his soul will transform these residual emotions through **YOUR** practice of it.

There is a link in your mutual past where you died for him and with him for a cause you both believed and were willing to die for. There really is no 'time', so though it seems it was a past life in human misperception, it is fresh, not old, a current vibratory experience, not past.

You courageously died with him, taking pleasure that your executioners would release you both together from that life you were in. Death was more favorable than the continuance of that life.

He carried the hatred, bitterness and sense of defeat over to the Guevara incarnation... you forgave the killers, he became one, justifying it behind a cause. His familiarity and fascination with the darker side of the human mind is to be illumined with love and forgiveness. This has nothing to do with the false love of an icon status from society. When you died, your love for him and forgiveness of your executioners were your last prevalent earthly thoughts. Although your soul so attuned to his through your love for him, did take on some of his rage and darkness. When he died with you, his last earthly thoughts were consumed by his desire to 'get even', his hatred of the situation and the people involved, and a strong desire to even the score at all costs of what he perceived as his personal defeat. Your connection with him and love for him had you take on and be born with those attributes that you both now work on to heal together from the different dimensions in which you currently exist. The separation of these dimensions is illusory from the human stand-point; it is all one within Creation. The healing and transformation of these residual attributes is an integral aspect of this union, which you both perceive as a mission. It is purpose, not 'a mission'. It is the continued expansive nature of Creation itself, living through your life experiences. You are simply aligned and resonating with your Divine nature, which is the nature of creation, inherent in every particle of all there is.

As there is no concept of 'time' other than on your earthly dimension, the essence of thought and the only reality that carries any power, or lack thereof, is **_what is_**. Thought has more power than humans can fathom.

He was born into his last incarnation within a supportive family. Those gifts were to be utilized for healing, but the residual thought forms he died with previously created his denial of the gifts and made the choice to get involved with and focus upon the illusions of politics and power disguised to fool his own true nature as 'helping the poor'. Therefore, he chose warfare as the means of change, blinding himself to other options available that would have had a different outcome. This was his dharma and it is not to be judged as heroic or evil, good or bad, it just is.

He became addicted to outsmarting the illusion of an 'enemy' **_outside himself_** and at all costs would act this out, even when circumstance was against him.

He died in that last incarnation with hatred, bitterness, betrayal, guilt and defeat, a repeated pattern of the past. This pattern he has seen through a disembodied clarity, thereby igniting a resonant vibration to heal, thereby attracting the resonant earthly being to assist in its healing transformation.

Though his ideals were manifested through darkness, their essence was seeded in light. This is a crux of the healing now being addressed for him---you resonated with his frequency. Creation's laws attract the resonating counterparts to each other through dynamic resonant frequencies for ascension and personal evolution toward Divine Light for all beings within Creation. Your earthly terms are soul-mate, twin-flame and a host of other such descriptions. None of us are alone."

Sunday 7:45 P.M.

The anticipation, ordering or ingesting a full meal fully evokes Vea. Full belly equals intense otherworldly bliss for him. With the exception of some meals in Europe, food has never had a very exciting effect on me, even with holiday feasts. I eat larger portions than I ever have when sharing my culinary experience with my revolutionary inhabitant, and the fullness afterward is total Vea occupation. I find this both amusing and endearing.

☆ THE BLISS OF THE CIGAR ☆

25 July

Woke up immersed in a powerful love, feeling the strength and vitality of Vea's presence.

...7:30 P.M.

The ecstasy of Vea's presence stayed with me all day. Began reading Goethe's poem "Reynard the Fox". Having several fine cigars remaining from the stash gifted me by my friend Callaway, I will partake in the pleasure of Goethe and a cigar.

26th of July

Mountain lion screamed before sleep last night, a powerful serenade into slumber.

DREAM: being driven in small, junk heap of an old car somewhere in Argentina. Che was the driver. He was messy and very sexy. We were driving through a 'locals' neighborhood with other tourists in the back seat. Some energy of danger seemed present to North Americans. I remember feeling ashamed to be so 'white' and from North America. I wanted to kiss him and be his woman with an unbearable intensity.

Dropping off the other tourists, we kissed heavily for a long time. Went to a local's home that he knew and he made passionate love to me.
I remember feeling like 'just another woman he did this with' and wanted it not to be so, craving him to actually want me in his life. I wanted desperately to impress him so he was attracted to me for more than just sex.
The intensity of kissing was beautiful and thrilling.

I had read about him in an online capitalist magazine, and some articles stated he was a filthy, smelly wimp who with all those guerillas of the time, were pretenders to battle and bravery.
The whole takeover of the regime by Fidel was 'bought' and the battles depicted were exaggerated and even staged. He had ordered the murder of thousands and he specialized in psychological torture of the prisoners.

Although I cannot support the horrors of warfare on any level, I cannot judge any soldier's actions, as they all are under the influence of something I will never understand.

As he lay on his deathbed, I remember asking my father about the war from the years he served in the army air corps. The horrific memories stirred back to life, his head reared up despite his debilitating weakness, his vacant eyes opened wide and filled with an emotion I've never seen in him as he said with the last bit of intensity he could muster, *"war is hell!"* He died the next day.

Full Moon, Sundown

"Evolution continues from all dimensions...manifesting through everything. As it manifested through Avea. . . she was given the name in Le Catedral and baptized at Iguazu...arrival in Argentina confirmed the absolute resonance of this one human 'seen' on the earth planet through the matrix from her light emanations and tonal frequencies.

She has grown into the union through the contrasting cycles of transition, integration with expansion into complete allowing and acceptance.

The movement has found its way to be focused as sunrays through micro glass. (magnifying glass)

She has accepted role of non-political evolutionary, same essence expressed through her polar opposite incarnation. . . health and empowerment- -she was incarnated for this and has stepped up, agreeing to keep eyes open through a life experience containing many earthly distractions. Those distractions served to strengthen the character, resolve and denial of personal defeat.

Holding the land with the water is key. This space is the sanctuary for the transformation we resonated with simultaneously. Being in her cellular matrix is ecstasy. Not to get lost in that, ever.

Full stomach. . . cigar creek side today. . .I named her and she, my ever, ever beloved accepted, trusts, understands. She let's me through. Does not doubt me to be **_not._** Earthly interruptions don't disrupt the flow but served to strengthen it.

She allows my healing of Che's lifetime...she gets through moments of judgment into not, of what she learns of Che ... so precious her motive to indulge my past pleasure of cigar smoke and mate', of which I care not; *but day-dreaming. . .* *this* a new gift for me she gives.

27 Julio
Friday, Sweet Friday 7 A.M.

I release all fears of success and notoriety.
Jeff and Ashton come to visit us from Arizona today
(husband and son of my pregnant niece who died by her own
hand).

* * *

Late afternoon
Creek side Cigar Ceremony

Smoked the first cigar sent from Callaway, my friend who
smokes only the Dominican Republic variety. Vea came forth
indubitably.

Sitting down at the creek alone with nature and my cigar.
Occasionally I used to smoke these things for fun with my
friend years ago. Callaway is a cigar connoisseur and only
smokes the best.
I used to inhale them then, I mean, how could you *NOT?* To
just swish smoke around your mouth and face seemed
absurd. It still does and I *still* inhale them.

I say aloud, "So if you're here, hold this thing as *you* di
few seconds lapse, when I'm not paying attention to '
my fingers reposition themselves around my smok·
companion. **Crazy as this sounds, the ci**
absolutely DELICIOUS.

I sucked on it and licked it. Turned it ro'
and tongue, which were wrapped arour
sucked it until it became fully warm
Smoke enveloped me. Thick, curly
private **- s u c c u l e n t** ·

The mind becomes en

Sitting here on a rock in the middle of the creek. Then standing, facing upstream to the 'v' shaped formation of the shore's edge of the island.

The sun is to my back, my silhouette on a tall rock stands before me. My shadow appears elongated, lean, beautiful, and shapely with the cigar in my hand. Shadows of the smoke swirl from the hand of my silhouette.

Many moments pass communing with emptiness and oneness with Vea.

The pungency of the smoking phallus makes this an erotic experience.

Just the ritual of it made it that much more
  pure & sensual -
        cigar smoking at its absolute finest.

On this rock mid-creek, the essence of him is all inside and within my cellular body and yet *not* me. It's thrilling to share my being on this level and feel the quality of love that is experienced from this 'union'.

It's from the *inside out*, this multidimensional lovemaking. The term 'lovemaking' is but a hint of remote similarity to the nest, deepest tantric human interaction connected with this m. It's off the bloody charts of any measurement or parison with two human bodies intermingling.

ar is down to 2 or 3 inches and is such a darkened to almost be black. I smoked the whole damn thing n here a couple of hours. Soul-delicious. The cigar has left a delicious scent upon my

Readying myself for the ascent up the hill, Kimberly's presence envelops me. (my niece on the other side) She asks if she can come to me. I can hear her cute voice with that NY accent. I, of course acquiesce.

"Please tell Jeff he's doin' good. I'm sorry. I miss you Jeff. I'm sorry you're alone, but I gave you our son and I had to leave. I'm sorry I just didn't see any way out of what I couldn't deal with. Love Ashton for me. I'm sorry I left you, Ashton."

At the moment her words fade, Ashton calls for me from up the hill. As I re-write this herein, emotions come over me and for a few seconds run through and envelope me.

28 Julio

Needing to daydream more and rest my overactive mind, I went to the creek yesterday afternoon indulging myself empty time.

Written in bed, still warm, cozy, only half awake and still *within the dream:*

His face so clear - Che, so much love with us. A little girl is hovering around us - is she ours? A very large man aiming a gun, Che kept ducking out of shot. Then the scene shifted instantly to us riding on an open-air train moving forward. Less bumpy than a truck and with train-like motion, I conclude us to be on rails not wheels.

Just when I thought we were safe, I was aimed at too. A loud blast, and Che was shot.
Next scene was calm as he lay dying in my arms.
The dream was in black & white, not color.

Fidel stabbed the shooter. We were all together on the train car. The shooter had big eyes, "dark with blood". Fidel keeps the bayonet in him hard, twisting it, pushing it. I see this clearly. The shooter's eyes were wide-open staring blank yet intensely, straight at me. It seemed a long time passed. The stabbed man falls over to the right. 'Fidel shot Che' – this being my immediate thought in the moment Fidel quickly stabbed this man.

Che was lying in my lap and I was huddled over him, our faces very close, I felt the warmth of his body and his breath. His head was cradled in my arms and his body off to my right. The child. "She will be safe with Fidel." I remember those being my thoughts, I also remember deep concern for the child in the instant I thought this.

The feeling of intense, deep and eternal love was clear. Che & I were in our own world untouched by any other thoughts, including his dying or that of the child.

The intensity of the love between us was all we were. "Don't worry, I'll be with you soon, my Love, we will NEVER part." This was a telepathic thought between us, neither of us spoke the actual words, but it was a knowing we shared and were enveloped within.

Upon waking and coming out of the visual part of this dream, the vibration of love resonating was more than I've ever felt in my waking life, save for my baby daughters when in those private, tender moments I thought I'd either burst or disappear from the intense love I felt for my babies.

I was filled with the unequivocal knowing: *"I was shown something – this was not a dream."* This 'knowledge' was above intellectual dispute of any kind, it was indeed, absolute. Emotion wells thru me in these very quiet moments.

I don't want to be separated from this, and I may never be.

There was too much love for there to be grief in those moments I held him before his life slipped away.

"Fidel used the man to shoot Che for *HIM*. The child & I would be cared for by Fidel." These were thoughts I had in the dream through a telepathic connection I was tuned into with Fidel at the same time I was holding my beloved.

As I began to waken, I was still holding Che, he was still alive, and we were sharing an unspoken love deeper than I ever dreamed love could be face to face. I held onto my slumberous state as I did not want to lose this moment, and as I passed to wakefulness he died in my arms.

Awesome Sunset 8:15 P.M.

Being alone on the land has lifted the last remaining veil between my current self and my life prior to this presence joining me.

This must be similar to the ecstatic state people have taken drugs to replicate. **I do not see how any substance can bring about this type of altered state of being.**

Black tea and a cigar on my deck with the lovely 'Futuro Tango' CD playing, sets the stage for a peaceful introspection of how the course of my life has completely changed since this presence has made itself known to be with me in both my waking and sleeping states.

The dream last night following the writing, and then being strongly 'directed' to get out of bed and put it into the computer was compelling.

The doorway, thus.

Smoking the larger, longer and lighter colored cigar with my evening tea. It *too* is delicious.

I am directed to *write, write, write.*
On the first of August, at the 11th hour post meridian, *the* 'direction' was fully realized.

The state of bliss was 'activated' within me in this time of reflection, and I have been altered yet again; more powerfully, and the light is brighter and somehow *crisper.*

There are moments of downright fun sharing my humanness and the senses therein with my non physical companion.

This light brown cigar is stronger than the small dark one I smoked down at the creek although still very sweet.

The sun has tucked down well beneath the horizon, leaving just a hint of itself with mauve overtones dimly illuminating my surroundings.

He's *pore-ing* out of me. I've only had glimpses of what now

simply *IS.*

Tango classes are planned for Saturday in Sacramento. F I N A L L Y !

A nervous system anything less than extremely robust could never accommodate such potent energy for sustained periods without frying the human host in some way.

This love flowing through me is amplified many-fold from the pale-by-comparison romance in the mortal-to-mortal/lust/maybe love this material world has ever provided. The flow of my endorphins when the presence baths me in ecstatic love is *over the top.*

It's getting quite dark, the tango music is so mellow and sensuous it compliments the sound of the trees swaying in the evening breezes.

I am in sustained ecstasy right now and can barely hold the pen. So much for an uneventful tea...

* * *

This cigar ritual is totally different than the creek side experience. Pick it up, suck on it and inhale a bit, setting it down in my clean ashtray for many moments and 'receive'. Be a blank mind, 'receive', then write what comes through without seeing the words on the paper as they are being written. Then pick the cigar up again and it's still smokin'. The breeze keeps enough airflow to keep it lit. Thank you Mother Nature dearest for your assistance.

Having to keep relighting it would be no fun and I wouldn't be doing it.

"The Awakening at Aravaipa", is a chapter in a book rather than an entire book about this initial multidimensionally awakening experience. That event paved the way for this current expansion of consciousness and has actually assisted me in understanding what happened way back then. Having had that event in my life assists me in understanding better what is happening now.

3 Agosto

My horse painting went to the fair today. It is my first official entry of an original art piece to be judged and possibly win something.

I don't want to get addicted to the ecstasy my ghost's presence brings and thereby feel empty and low when it's not flowing through me, intoxicating me. The breaks actually give my nervous system a rest. I feel it to be a potent day finishing my pathway in the garden between my cabin and my daughter's home. Not inspired to write. Blank mind.

Moments later....

Back inside from chilly deck side teatime. Giving myself some moments to be empty before the fullness of my day begins. The ecstasy returns, I'm in it now. These moments are not about the book, writing, anything.
Vea and me. Being one in this body. That's all there is and all else dissolves into nothing. Nada.

No point in manifesting into another body when the ultimate love is all contained within this one.

Sex is the act of becoming one with each other for mortal lovers. I remember those days. Vea and I are already one. *This is the ultimate love.*

4 Agosto

Vea speaks of a friend whose name I will not mention, but as it is a direct communication from him, I will write his words. I receive this as I was contemplating the shift in my friend's energy:

"Beware of the tides of friendship turning, as she has buried deep the negative feelings of jealousy that she is not even conscious of having toward you. This can become more than she can hide. She's not aware of this, or if she IS, she is denying them and feeling guilty because of them."

This received information I found interesting, and could judge as disturbing, but I tend to not have judgments on received information as I have on my own thought patterns. Received information evokes feelings, not judgments. Received information is pure, my thoughts can be and usually are clouded or deceptive in some way.

Tango today in Sacramento. Very excited to finally be surrounding myself with the music and dance of Argentina with others. To immerse myself in this long missed ambience.

5 Agosto
Sunday 7 A.M.

"You did not go there to learn 'how' to dance tango. You got what you went for in the first moments only...think about this."

This above channeled message came through in what I learned is called 'automatic writing' when I awakened in the wee hours, still very sleepy.

Tango. In the beginning of the first class and the end of the second, the higher energies were brought in by Oscar the beautiful, Argentine tango champion dance instructor. His equally gorgeous wife, Georgina says in her beautiful accent, " Your body is the whole orchestra. Feel and play all the instruments." I was mesmerized.

"Why *me*, why do you come through *me* Vea? The Argentine tango couple is so beautiful, their culture so rich. *Why me- -* a 52-year-old white woman in North America? My frustration and sadness beckoning forth as I indulge in self pity.

"Because the culture, the country, does not matter. It is the openness of mind and *allowance of the situation*. Becoming the situation. The link. The love. Tango and skin color matters not, language, not. This could not have occurred with any one younger. Youth and old age are illusory passages. Earth years are irrelevant in Spirit.

It's the open heart...receiving, sustaining, and remembering a love that only seems like it was in the distant past. That distant past is only from the limited, microscopic, human misperception. This is the crux of the teaching. Human perception of soul mates is humorous. It's not about having sex, having babies, domesticity.

Two bodies embraced in lovemaking are just attempting to experience where we are now. Being together inside one body, experiencing simultaneous *everything*. Emotions, satisfying hunger with a sensational meal, true oneness from *WITHIN*. Our thoughts are one! Your pleasure is my pleasure, your pain is my pain, your bliss is my bliss and it's exponential now. That IS why your highs have been so high and your lows so low and your anger so intense when it arises...because it's times two. Forget the fantasy of your Zorro character coming to the door being Vea... you would be too distracted by form. Forget the lovely Latino man coming into your life, you would be too distracted by form.

No distraction to the essence of what we have comes from me being inside your body...after the integration process, I know was like giving birth. The labor and pain was mind opening not cervix, (the opposite chakra), your energetic upset will mellow...our integration will bring us both gifts we would not have with two separate bodies.

We must be both consciously inside one to herald in the vibrational healing at the level it is and needs to be. It needs to come through a being in complete oneness with love. Che's healing on the other dimension brings him to Vea. Kari's healing here brings her to Ave. This vibrational oneness, consciously integrated brings us to AVEA.
Mergence...the light worker that is effective en masse, has fully embraced the darkness. No fear. Our resonance joined us and sustains us."

"THIS UNION HEALS YOU BOTH. THE PROCESS *ITSELF* IS THE BLISS."
(this one line informational transmission came during the dialog I was receiving from Vea, then Vea's communication continued as follows)

"A beautiful tango connection dance pales in comparison. An exquisite lovemaking between mortals also pales by comparison. Both are the human attempts at experiencing what we now have and human reflections of the divinity you are now experiencing, and I am now experiencing through you."

5 Agosto
Sunday Night

Tango. Initially, I was in heaven with their accent, the music, and the language. When we students were individually taught 'the connection' of tango and explained the 'life' of tango I felt myself to be in exactly the right place. The young Argentine couple was so beautiful it brought tears to my eyes. Their passion was electric. **I was moved to the core.**

Then as the dance practice began, my dream space was jerked into blatant frustration at having to go through the steps with an assortment of partners who not only knew nothing about the *feeling* of such a dance, but also were the usual 'stiff', uptight American male.

I felt Vea's presence strong during the initial experience, learning of the tango connection before being directed to couple with others and learn the steps.

My first partner, due to a shortage of males, was a woman a bit older than myself. She was well poised, beautiful and had lovely energy. I thoroughly enjoyed the steps with her, as that part of the lesson entailed only establishing *the connection heart to heart,* and had nothing to do with the steps of the dance itself. I felt Vea enjoy this as did I.

It was straight downhill from there and I had to curtail my overwhelming urge to bolt out of the place. I endured both classes leaving at the end quite disappointed at having been left standing alone and invisible after everyone found a partner to practice with. Even the instructors did not acknowledge my solitary presence and come to my rescue teaching me what I came there to learn. Determined, I moved to the music pretending to have a partner just to move my feet according to the assigned steps and spare myself the humiliation of standing in the middle of the floor, the only one without a partner, not dancing.

✶ HONESTY OF INNOCENCE ✶

On the deck early this morning I had a fabulous visit with little Emma after her trip. She was telling me about Disneyland in her adorable little voice full of expression. During her visit, I was still feeling very altered from the intensity of the prolonged ecstatic blending with the presence.

This altered state had been ongoing since the family left several days before and I was alone on the property. Emma looks at me and says matter-of-factly, "Ima, there's a scary man on your face." She told me she didn't like this and asked, "Who *is* that scary man on your face, Ima?" She could not give me a description as to what she saw, but when we went in the cabin and she saw the face of Ernesto on the cover of "The Motorcycle Diaries", she recognized it as being the man on my face and exclaimed it matter of factly.

The honesty of what an innocent child states unprovoked is something to pay attention to, especially something of this nature that seems totally abstract.

9 Agosto

My vocal apparatus *craves* speaking Spanish. I recite days of the week, and months of the year just to *feel it and hear it* and roll my tongue.

Last night's dinner out had a violin concerto playing that mi papa played when I was a child. He'd play that piece on his beloved violin that I have now, when I was going to sleep - such a wonderful memory. Emotion moved me this morning overflowing with gratitude for the gifts from those memories my father gave me.

12 Agosto

Woke to Emma knocking. New morning ritual: she knocks on the door, climbs into bed with me for one minute and then goes home.

Read the alleged 'truthful' extent of Che Guevara's actions and mind-thought. Some of his reported actions seem to reflect a potentially diseased mind.

That book sent by Callaway, the latest one out: *"Exposing the Real Che Guevara and the Useful Idiots who Idolize Him"* by *Humberto Fontova* is an eye opener for anyone who might be under the influence of the iconic exaltations of Sr. Guevara. His actions display betrayal to his youthful idealistic dreams for rescuing innocent peoples from poverty and exploitation.

Have I been duped? This love I've felt, is it even possible for such love to come from a soul with this darkness or am I being totally used? Am I just another *useful idiot*?
Does this soul truly need this situation with ME to evolve?
Doubts again flood my mind. Are we using *each other?*

No? That the energy is present in my life is not a fabrication of my mind, of this I am sure.

Does the death transition make that personality see their wrongs and instill a wish to repent? Is this his repentance and I his conduit to earth? Death does not provide instant all-knowing enlightenment..or does it? The only thing that rings true is that the transition is no doubt different for each soul, as is their life, as are their fingerprints.

Now I fully understand why a person who's older, wiser, in possession of a mind open to more than what it just sees, knows or perceives and never heard of Che Guevara was necessary for this situation to occur.

Now it is my time to correct my judgments and forgive him the atrocities and brutality he's committed on such a large scale in that last incarnation that I've just read. And I must forgive myself the painful patterns I've called into my life and repeated unconsciously. Time to move forward. Time to accelerate toward the light of the one true Source and rise above the continued earthly distractions that have plagued my human experience.

Time to leave behind the monuments I've built with my emotions.

Will I actually say 'yes' to his desire to come through me and expose myself to the live families who have suffered deeply for so long since his terrorization of them? He does, after all, wish to express his sincere remorse for the pain he caused them. Am I to deny him this due to my own fears or wishes to keep our union to myself?

Che received adoration from a global population in his lifetime, some still adore him because he was handsome, charismatic and iconized by the media! If not for his good looks, this phenomenon may not have occurred. This illustrates the danger of the mindset of groupies that don't want to know the truth behind their idol's pretty face. Some wear that famous tee shirt and don't know the name of the person who's face with the riveting stare is wearing that beret.

Castro and Che are portrayed as two monsters, one alive and one dead. One martyred by the one who allegedly set up his death and so easily used his knowledge of him against him. Then he stole his family (?) Who will ever know the truth behind all this? Does it even matter?

Vea's input:

"I do not want the hero worship for the incarnation of Che Guevara. I want people to grow within and hold court in their OWN minds and hearts for truth and honor. The media can invent and/or be fed absolute shit and turn their heads from the truth, thereby leading the masses to do the same. Unfortunately, the populace eats up the media contrived lies. Cowardice, brutality and bullshit, and it's still going on in full force. The Cubans are dealt the same hand as were the Jews and all other peoples being terrorized and exploited throughout this world currently as they have been throughout history.

Somehow, my assistance to correct this is a mission to rectify the mistakes I have made for a belief I blindly followed and in so doing inflicted suffering on so many. The correction of mistakes applying forgiveness, not blame, is the path all humans should undertake, whether they be in lowly positions or positions of power. This is the first step to healing the mass disease of the human species. The inability to forgive and allow people to live without this age old need to control and exert power for the sake of greed for one's own personal gain is epidemic and is the demise of quality of life and ultimately of life itself.

The freedom and courage people long to honor, need to be projected onto Gandhi, Mother Teresa and others who practiced non-violence and compassion. Che Guevara became self-righteous behind a belief system he thought he needed for his own fulfillment, which was a disguise for his own fears of inadequacy. This ego-based fear system fooled him into thinking he was implementing a greater good for the masses. Blessed leadership capabilities and a charismatic presence- those gifts were mis-used to feed the overdeveloped fear filled small man and under-developed spirit, which possessed no knowledge of its own empowerment.

I wish to give to the world and the survivors of my brutality, *my honest and absolute apology* for my misuse of power and the suffering it caused. *This was no example to follow.* I wish to apologize for those actions and the voice that allows this to come forth is through Ave. I gave her the name and she had the courage to take it and grow into it and present to the world what came through her from me. *I maintain promotion of the evolution of the spirit and for individuals to become revolutionaries for their own empowerment.*

Do not harm, hate or discredit Ave. She is NOT ME, although she allowed the integration of our energies into her personal matrix and makes the deliverance of this information the priority I request. She agreed to be my voice to each and every victim of the heinous crimes against humanity by my hand, directly or indirectly from my life as Che Guevara. To issue forth an apology in words that are inadequate to convey, *I seek not forgiveness for my own sake or any continued adoration.* I wish the voices of those victims be heard, that they may be set free from their continued suffering when they witness this continued idol worship of a face that does not warrant or deserve this honor.

The image should represent what NOT to be, what NOT to worship. I made mistakes in the name of what I thought to be the highest good at the time. My ideals were funneled through a series of mistakes, and drunken on the illusion of power and courage my mistakes were justified in my limited thought-processes. I was blinded and intoxicated with righteousness.

The creed currently recited by the children in the Cuban schools should never again be uttered. **The creed should be regarding empowerment of the self for the highest good for everyone.**

The Che Guevara propaganda machine, still fed and propagated should be stamped off the face of the earth and in its place utilize that energy to teach the highest human ideals...
courage, freedom and individual empowerment, proper nutrition and spiritual awakening.

Let the image of 'your idol' represent a spiritual revolution from **within the individual.**

12 Agosto

"I cannot repair the damage done.
I cannot undo the crimes committed against many people. . .
I rode in on the pure love that is
  inherent in even the most outwardly evil
            of human potential.

          I can only encourage all of you
in love with the image of what I thought myself to be, to seek
and **read truth behind lies**.
        Focus the outpouring of energies onto
    healing the survivors of my cruelty and the
    innocent descendants who are now enslaved in
their own country because of the beast
  I helped create.   Shift your view of my image
      from what you look up to be as a man of courage and let
it rather represent the hypocrisy
        of idol worship...let it serve to remind you
      to develop your own natural empowerment.
  Know that my image was used as all media is
used---
      to twist the truth to its opposite and sold
    to the masses who long for an empowered,
                enlightened leader.

The empowerment and enlightenment you seek
in another lies within each of you.
Look not outside yourself. Eat not the lies
you are fed.
Do not hold further resentment for having eaten
of the lies, release it and feed upon it
no longer."

<u>Sunday Night</u>
<u>August 12/13,</u>
<u>12:05 AM, Monday</u>

This day spent typing all the journals from Argentina into my computer for this book, taking breaks only to color with my little Emma.

Today I asked Emma again about the man on my face, if it was still there. She said it was not still there and was adamant about him being there only the other day. I put the book away from her original recognition and the skeptic in me wanted to test her further - so I showed her the 'El Che' calendar I brought home from B.A. and thumbed through the months. I'd say, "him?" she'd say "no", until I arrived at a particular month, and she said, "it's him, *that's* the man." She was very sure of her choice. She didn't know all the pictures were of the same man in different poses, expressions and moods. The picture she had selected was one where his expression was soft and gentle, not that of the more tough-guy revolutionary with the Latino-machisistic personality he was known to have possessed.

Typing my journal entries into the computer with the intent purpose on the publication of this experience with my invisible companion finds me finally at peace. It's a peace knowing I am functioning within an actual purpose.

The Pigeon Chronicle's illustrations are a close second in evoking this peace of harmonious purpose. But I must say, there is an undertone of trepidation to make public something as personal and abstract as my journals of this life and expansive experience.

It's very strange when something outside of me can read my mind and I'm aware of it. **Multidimensional telepathy.**

It is unexplainably strange, yet not unpleasant, when I sense my thoughts are being shared by another, and my most private moments are no longer absolutely private, but being sensed and shared by someone both from within me and also outside me simultaneously.

He hovers outside me *and* inhabits my body at seeming random times. He utilizes my senses to enjoy the experience of eating, breathing and walking outside in nature. He has assisted me with the tasks of splitting wood and cleaning the chimney top when it becomes clogged with creosote, up on the roof during a pouring rain in the middle of the night.

I can thoroughly enjoy his company and inhabitation now that the fears of being insane have passed and I accept his presence in my life as actual. I haven't been self-conscious at his company when he is with me in private moments. Sometimes, the intensity of his energy merging with mine within my body has caused uncomfortable spasms not unlike some sort of electrical charge. Luckily this does not happen when anyone else is present.

Needless to say, I keep personal company with no mortal man for any reason.

My friend who sends me cigars knows also of this experience with Che Guevara and is more or less curiously entertained by the story. He invited me on his "Earth Mysteries" radio show and interviewed me regarding this experience. He also mailed me the new book "Exposing The Real Che Guevara".

This book was riveting and put light onto the dark effects the propaganda machine had set in motion way back during the days when Che Guevara was alive. It seems based on factual recounts of family members of the victims and those that survived some of the beastly tortures themselves.

Facts that were of course denied, covered up or glossed over, dazzling the public with a fabrication of acts of a man who's claim to fame was his looks, charisma and the bullshit fed to society. Society loves to eat bullshit, and if presented with facts, will still choose the side dish of bullshit over a nutritional meal of truth.

I became quite upset with the information in this book. I started to again judge my ghost from his past life, not from who he is after shedding that persona, and experienced another round of cleansing from the beast of judgment.

Unlike others who may have read the censored books written by this 'deeply, philosophical, idealist' and defend his iconic status, I experienced feeling rather angry. I could not get out from under the blanket of judging him to be a full-fledged, mentally ill bastard, but worse, my abhorrence for the propaganda machine that dupes the public on a regular basis, and continues to do so using a variety of characters.

I'm choosing the nutritional meal of truth; I've had it with bullshit...never did like the taste or smell of it. I don't know quite how to deal with my conflicting feelings after reading this book and having 'felt' and communicated directly with the spiritual entity, which is actually no longer embodied in that infamous life.
He's still intense, even now. He's also so very loving, and receiving his love has been the sweetest thing I've ever known. The rapture I have experienced from the ecstasy he has bestowed is undeniably the essence of divine nectar itself, what people strive for when romance begins with another. This is a love story of healing and spiritual expansion within a sacred multidimensional union.

Ironic how my previous romantic partnership with a mortal had reeled me in on his charisma, power and his popular reputation with many who knew him, then as time went by and we settled in together, the dark side of his charismatic personality came out and I suffered from it as long as I chose to be with him.

13 Agosto

Neal's brother died of a heart attack Saturday night. Dean was a year younger than ME and I *knew* him! Knowing Neal for more than half my life and being my closest friend on the planet for that long, I find my own self altered from the state of shock that Neal is no doubt in. Further 'proof' of energetic connections even with one both far away in distance, lifestyle and infrequent communication.

My Aunt Elaine introduced me to sudden death and its energetic repercussions with the bursting of an undetected aneurysm. My best friend's young son dying of a heart condition diagnosed as non-life-threatening, and my pregnant niece introduced me to the tragedy of suicide of ones we deem too young to die.

I am well acquainted with the altered zombie state of being the surviving relative. When my father died from his illness at 77, it was not shocking, but the grief was still a very real 'passage' and his was my initial introduction to the transition we call death 20 years ago. On his deathbed he managed the energy to show me the bowing of Mozart's 5th concerto; that was his final request of me, to learn this piece on his violin.

I had been sporting a newly altered state on a very private level between Vea and myself after reading that book by Fontova. Word of the sudden death of my friend's brother added to that status.

This limbo went on for several days, but I maintained my intent to be set upon growing and settling with all of it, realizing these events to be another door to be opened leading to my own inner light-source and authentic self. *Man,* it's a long and winding road!

15 Agosto

I still feel intense love despite what I have learned in this book regarding the actions and choices of my ghost's past incarnation. Tonight I felt tenderness and was 'filled' with the knowledge of how all beings are pure love when stripped of their human flaws.

Yesterday when I stroked my face and neck, it felt as if someone else was in my fingertips providing the caress. It felt different than when I touch my own face and neck in the same way.

'My ghost' was clearly touching me, and I felt his love, tenderness and appreciation come *through* my own fingertips. The quality of the touch was from one who was not actually me, but one who loved me. This was too clear to be misinterpreted as something from my own imaginative delusion.

It was as obvious a sensory distinction between rubbing your own neck when tense, and feeling the hands of a masseur's healing touch.

18 Agosto

The scent of citrus tree blossoms is intoxicating. The miniature lemon trees left from the wedding, still decked in their wide, shiny, pink ribbons now blowing in the breeze emanate their fragrance and bring me great olfactory joy.

My eldest daughter outside in her yard, I see her from the distance and find myself intoxicated with yet another 'fragrance'. This is the fragrance of motherhood come full circle. The pleasure of seeing the grace of my daughter in her movements and extreme beauty, brings me unparalleled joy.

The pleasure of either of my daughters' company has the power to uplift me still. A gift from the Divine Creative Source to lay my eyes upon them, have a quality interaction with them, and live my life in close proximity to them both.

And now there's the addition of Emma! The Divine placement of the part of life's path I am upon currently makes itself apparent through the relationships I have with my daughters and now my granddaughter.

No matter what else I achieve or don't achieve, have or don't have, possess or don't possess, I am LIVING the greatest of human gifts.

A butterfly the size of a hummingbird that is flying out in the yard at a distance has just circled quickly and flew over me in more of a dart than a flutter, leaving a line of luminescent energy over my head that lasted a few seconds. I love living out in nature as she gives so much. I share this with Vea, whose last incarnation provided no joy out in nature as he stalked and was stalked by the perceived enemy.

Awakened today with no immediate memory of last night's channeled musical experience, but after some moments, I had total recollection. I played my violin as never before for a very long time, and played the keyboard as if I had for years. (I don't even play keyboard, except this one I'm typing on!) This musical experience was my private requiem honoring Neal's brother.

My shoulder didn't hurt at all with the intense and ongoing bowing of the violin and doesn't hurt this morning either. First time in awhile I haven't felt the presence of discomfort in my shoulder.

21 Agosto

Feeling a bit of yearning to be physically held by my ghost. I wish he'd materialize for just one evening for dinner and a romp in the hay. So much for the extinguishing of *all* my human yearnings! This yearning is delicious though.

In bed early, I want to 'climb inside' and just feel myself within the physical embrace of my ghost. **Such love, *such love!***

22 Agosto

Going into seclusion with Vea and our book project. I am called to do this. Social engagements are cancelled other than family time and occasional dinner engagements, justified by still having to actually EAT.

This book will be treated like labor and delivery. **Nothing but this shall consume me.**

27 Agosto

Twenty years ago today marks the death of my father. A strange emotion defying explanation set in toward late afternoon and built up steam.

A brief early evening visit with Emma, we have peaches, blueberries and a glass of milk; her visits erase any upheaval of emotions from the moment she appears at my door, until she leaves, my deepest and darkest moods lift in her presence. She is simply, a precious light of love.

I've been sensing death energy. Thinking it to be my own, whenever this has happened it's always been a family member. Perhaps its just because it's the anniversary of my father's death.

No waves of ecstasy, no hits of intense and prolonged waves of love. Withdrawal from this natural high leaves me neutral and without disappointment or yearning. Acceptance and ease feel good.

30 Agosto

Sometimes I feel him standing behind my left shoulder as I sit at the table and put my journal entries into the computer.

31 Agosto
...11:11 P.M.

Home from a lovely evening visit with my old friend Douglas, we viewed two movies: Don Juan DeMarco and Assassination Tango, two awesome movies selected by my friend honoring the focus in my life with Che.

Che came to me during the evening's entertainment, subtle, yet unmistakable.

Watching tango *stirs* me.

Don Juan De Marco was wonderfully portrayed and very well produced. When I heard in this movie, "a soul splits in two on the way to earth, then one half finds the other half and that is how you can explain the phenomenon of love at first sight", a spark lit within me remembering that moment I first laid eyes on the image of Che, what was evoked, and the amazing awakening that brought my life to the delicious place it is.

Vea is *that* with me. That is how I learned of Avea. I am Ave he is Vea, we are 'Avea'-when the two are joined back into one.

✶ ✶ ✶

epilogue

i have been lead down an unexpected fork
on the path leading to my authentic self.
you, vea are an integral part of my authenticity
or i would not have been lead to you. we resonated,
integrated, expanded beyond what we
each were before our sacred union.

i am grateful, in retrospect, to have been
distracted from publishing
The PigeonChronicles, as my story was not up to
speed with the quality and beauty of my illustrations.
now i get to make that book into the masterpiece it
is destined to be as i rewrite the story from my newly
expanded self.
thank you, dear vea, for joining me and continuing with
me on this path of awakening to the fullness of our being! We
are the power of L O V E !

"The sacred texts I have studied and put into practice are too numerous to mention, and my path has been one of focus on impeccability. These studies have lead me to realize the purpose of mastering my own vibration. Maintaining vibrational mastery requires constant vigilance, awareness and observation of the emotional indicator system, for one's vibrational resonance calls forth the components that compose our life experience."

Ave is an artist, musician, songwriter, Kirtan singer, photographer, mother, nutritional and healthy lifestyle consultant, grandmother, mystic and global traveler, experiencing other cultures and ways of life that would be considered daring, courageous and downright revolutionary. She has several apprenticeships in an assortment of healing modalities, including but not limited to communications with animals and beings in the non-physical dimension. She is a recognized expert in the field of multi-dimensional communications.

Ave is currently recording a new genre of music that came to her in a flash of inspiration during one of her meditations based on the series presented by Oprah Winfrey and Deepak Chopra. She was directed to call this new music "Mantra Music" – Sanskrit mantras put to light electronic instrumentation incorporating her acoustic violin in the mix. This calling has resulted in the series being produced currently and the first part of the series is now available as her gift of healing and ease back to the world.

Ave is also called forth to write the sequel to this book, what her life has become after the integration of not only the energetic matrix of Vea, but of Infinite Intelligence in the form of 'received wisdom'.

Special Note To You, the Reader of this book:

It is also the intent of this book to assist others who may be receiving wisdom from the non-physical dimension, be it from departed family members, ascended masters, or other forms of information for guidance that are out of the spectrum of human understanding. Sharing this experience, it is my hope, to relieve the human receiving this wisdom from any doubts of their sanity, to know beyond the shadow of a doubt, there is no such thing as the demise of the human spirit once it transitions into non-physical.

There is much wisdom to be imparted, and those that have departed wish their beloved families to know they are still present and available for communication at any time. Their biggest frustration and source of sadness is to see their living relatives grieve continuously, feeling a loss that does not exist, thinking their loved ones are dead and gone. Through this book, may you be awakened to the new and deeper relationship possibilities that extend beyond the five senses.

Feel ease in being open to knowing that life continues on unseen dimensions that can be accessed by humans, as we are equipped to be 'receivers' of both love and information that is always available for our well-being and spiritual expansion.

Author's note about Ernesto Che Guevara:

Whatever Che Guevara was in that lifetime,
    he has shared with me profound love and
        compassion, expanded his resonance through the many
healing sessions he and I shared, bringing about my own healing
and expansion.   I was ripe and resonating with
        the source being of his beautiful essence,
    and he found me to be the one he trusted to
            bring his message from the other side.

My love and Sincere Gratitude go to my daughters, Brandy
and Amelya, who have always encouraged my creativity.

Thank you also, my dear circle of friends who have
supported me always, especially during the process of
living this book and then writing it.

My love and deepest appreciation goes to
Robbi Spencer, my creative partner in my musical projects,
the creation and continuing expansion of my beautiful
website, my #1 support person with all aspects, spiritual,
technical and otherwise so I may bring my inspired ideas
into creation and offer it with love, to the world.
Robbi, I couldn't have done this without you! Thank you
for sharing with me your genius-wizard-abilities on so
many levels, and for your enduring friendship.

I wish to acknowledge, last but not least, my gratitude for having found the wisdom brought to me by Esther-Hicks and her non-physical group of Infinite Intelligence. Years after my integration with Che/Vea, did I discover this wisdom, delivered lovingly and with great humor.

Through hearing this wisdom I have had my experience validated beyond the shadow of any doubts I ever held, and although I wish I found it during my search for answers during this experience initially, I realize everything comes to us in perfect timing. Esther's relationship with her departed husband, Jerry Hicks, has identical components to my relationship experience with Che, right down to us enjoying our meals together!

One afternoon sitting on my terrace, I was joined by Che, Jerry Hicks and Abraham, and together they directed me to make a video and send it to Esther, I told them *"no way"* – Jerry said, "she's expecting it" – they said they wanted to all come through me and bring a new color of wisdom and guidance and call themselves "Chebraham" – and I can tell you, they thought they were very funny.

Nothing is more entertaining than sitting at a table with a group of beings in non-physical hearing their 'laughter' and feeling their merriment. I just said, "very funny, guys!"

At this juncture of time, I haven't made that video, but I also remember when Che told me to publish my journals of our transformational journey of love and healing and I said to him, "NO WAY!"

Their big, smiling retort in unison was,

"It will be revolutionary!"

SACRED GROVE
PUBLISHING

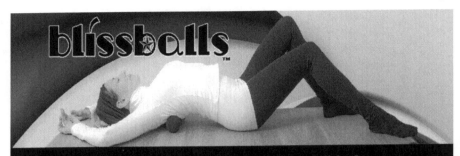

"Well being is the order of everything"
Abraham Hicks

One of the healing arts that I share is simple and FUN. The good feelings brought about by fun are indeed the basis of many a healing. Having fun or the lack of it shows up in many forms, emotionally and physically. Are you a 'fun person' or a 'serious person'? The saying, "laughter is the best medicine" rings true, yes? Of course most of us have had the sense of fun either programmed completely out of our resonant field or toned down considerably. This is the difference between children that play and the adults that work far more than they play. The command, "grow up!" was not delivered in the best interest of our well-being.

SO, FOLLOW YOUR BLISS! This may sound cliché, but in this aspect, just grab four tennis balls, put them in a sock and roll around on them. I'm calling this little life changing object BLISSBALLS™, because when you use them regularly, you will begin sighing in bliss when the tension releases and EASE begins to make itself known to you. Do you even remember feeling EASE rather than tension in your neck, shoulders or back?

Use your body weight for the pressure to make them dig in to those stuck places that hurt. It's not the balls that are causing the discomfort that you may feel when it rolls over certain spots, it's your body that is glued and all sticky and stuck from tension, and rolling around on these balls is unsticking it. How comfortable was it over the years leaning over the computer or whatever repetitive motion you've done to make that area stiff even when you're not doing the action that caused it? Well, it's going to take regular BLISS SESSIONS to release this pent up stress that took YEARS to accumulate, so be patient and keep at it.

The first time I rolled over these balls in the hip area, it was so painful I couldn't stand it....I didn't even know I had stuck energy here, but we all do, we just don't realize it until it is touched. A massage therapist with strong hands cannot access the areas within the hip area that these balls can reach, so just know that the more it hurts, the more the area NEEDS it.

Now, if you have an injury or surgical procedure, use common sense and don't irritate that particular area with using these balls when the healing process is still taking place. Use intuition, common sense and patience, three positive attributes built in to our human wiring and not always recognized as being valid guidance systems to our usually mindless routines. So using these BLISSBALLS™ will also assist in developing these three valuable aspects to enhance your entire life!!!

YourBlissBalls.com

NEW MANTRA MUSIC

In addition to being a published author and accomplished fine arts photographer, painter and illustrator, Ave has been expressing inspiration through the musical arts in various forms through the different phases of her life.

Her most recent projects include a CD of what she terms "Mantra Music" that is being created and produced with her long term creative partner, Robbi Spencer at SE Studios.

The video on the left is an example of the new "Mantra Music" CD. The first two tracks of this new music can be purchased by clicking on one of the album covers on the right to go to iTunes. Ave and Robbi are still creating new tracks that will soon be available.

It is our hope that this music transforms your life the way it has brought about ease and transformation in ours....our gift to you!

GET THE NEW MUSIC

AVE GUEVARA

COSMIC DESIRE

AVE GUEVARA

Je Suis Divinité

Available Now!